THIS BOOK BELONGS TO:

_____

_____

INDEX

INDEX

CHEESE *Tasting*

NAME		
CREAMERY		AGE
RIND		DATE
ORIGIN		PRICE

🥛 MILK

- ☐ Cow
- ☐ Sheep
- ☐ Goat
- ☐ Buffalo
- ☐ Raw
- ☐ _____

🧀 SMELL & TEXTURE

- ☐ Strong
- ☐ Medium
- ☐ Slight
- ☐ Odorless
- ☐ Runny
- ☐ Soft
- ☐ Semi-soft
- ☐ Semi-firm
- ☐ Firm
- ☐ Hard

📝 NOTES

Appearance:
_____
_____
_____

Aroma:
_____
_____
_____

Taste:
_____
_____
_____

Mouthfeel:
_____
_____
_____

😊 FLAVOR WHEEL

Earthy — Sharp/Tangy — Buttery/Creamy — Herbal — Salty — Nutty — Toasty — Caramel — Moldy/Blue — Grassy — Robust — Sour — Bitter — Fruity — Milky/Lactic — Sweet

👍 RATING ☆☆☆☆☆

🍷 COMBINED WITH

💬 COMMENTS/SUGGESTIONS
_____
_____
_____
_____
_____
_____
_____
_____
_____
_____
_____
_____

1

CHEESE Tasting

NAME	
CREAMERY	AGE
RIND	DATE
ORIGIN	PRICE

🥛 MILK

- ☐ Cow
- ☐ Goat
- ☐ Raw
- ☐ Sheep
- ☐ Buffalo
- ☐ _____

🧀 SMELL & TEXTURE

- ☐ Strong
- ☐ Medium
- ☐ Slight
- ☐ Odorless
- ☐ Runny
- ☐ Soft
- ☐ Semi-soft
- ☐ Semi-firm
- ☐ Firm
- ☐ Hard

📝 NOTES

Appearance:
_____
_____
_____

Aroma:
_____
_____
_____

Taste:
_____
_____
_____

Mouthfeel:
_____
_____
_____

😋 FLAVOR WHEEL

Earthy, Sharp/Tangy, Buttery/Creamy, Sweet, Herbal, Milky/Lactic, Fruity, Salty, Bitter, Nutty, Sour, Toasty, Robust, Caramel, Grassy, Moldy/Blue

😊 RATING ☆☆☆☆☆

🍷 COMBINED WITH

💬 COMMENTS/SUGGESTIONS

_____
_____
_____
_____
_____
_____
_____
_____
_____
_____
_____
_____
_____

2

CHEESE Tasting

NAME	
CREAMERY	AGE
RIND	DATE
ORIGIN	PRICE

🥛 MILK

- ☐ Cow
- ☐ Goat
- ☐ Raw
- ☐ Sheep
- ☐ Buffalo
- ☐ _____

🧀 SMELL & TEXTURE

- ☐ Strong
- ☐ Medium
- ☐ Slight
- ☐ Odorless
- ☐ Runny
- ☐ Soft
- ☐ Semi-soft
- ☐ Semi-firm
- ☐ Firm
- ☐ Hard

📝 NOTES

Appearance:
_____
_____
_____

Aroma:
_____
_____
_____

Taste:
_____
_____
_____

Mouthfeel:
_____
_____
_____

😊 FLAVOR WHEEL

Earthy — Sharp/Tangy — Buttery/Creamy — Herbal — Salty — Nutty — Toasty — Caramel — Moldy/Blue — Grassy — Robust — Sour — Bitter — Fruity — Milky/Lactic — Sweet

👍 RATING | ☆ ☆ ☆ ☆ ☆

🧀 COMBINED WITH

💬 COMMENTS/SUGGESTIONS

_____
_____
_____
_____
_____
_____
_____
_____
_____
_____
_____

CHEESE Tasting

NAME

CREAMERY	AGE
RIND	DATE
ORIGIN	PRICE

🥛 MILK

- ☐ Cow
- ☐ Goat
- ☐ Raw
- ☐ Sheep
- ☐ Buffalo
- ☐ _____

🧀 SMELL & TEXTURE

- ☐ Strong
- ☐ Medium
- ☐ Slight
- ☐ Odorless

- ☐ Runny
- ☐ Soft
- ☐ Semi-soft
- ☐ Semi-firm

- ☐ Firm
- ☐ Hard

📝 NOTES

Appearance:
_____
_____
_____

Aroma:
_____
_____
_____

Taste:
_____
_____
_____

Mouthfeel:
_____
_____
_____

😊 FLAVOR WHEEL

Earthy — Sharp/Tangy — Buttery/Creamy — Herbal — Salty — Nutty — Toasty — Caramel — Moldy/Blue — Grassy — Robust — Sour — Bitter — Fruity — Milky/Lactic — Sweet

⭐ RATING ☆☆☆☆☆

🍷 COMBINED WITH

💬 COMMENTS/SUGGESTIONS

_____
_____
_____
_____
_____
_____
_____
_____
_____
_____
_____
_____
_____

4

CHEESE Tasting

NAME		
CREAMERY	**AGE**	
RIND	**DATE**	
ORIGIN	**PRICE**	

🥛 MILK

- ☐ Cow
- ☐ Sheep
- ☐ Goat
- ☐ Buffalo
- ☐ Raw
- ☐ _____

🧀 SMELL & TEXTURE

- ☐ Strong
- ☐ Runny
- ☐ Firm
- ☐ Medium
- ☐ Soft
- ☐ Hard
- ☐ Slight
- ☐ Semi-soft
- ☐ Odorless
- ☐ Semi-firm

📝 NOTES

Appearance:
_____
_____
_____
_____

Aroma:
_____
_____
_____
_____

Taste:
_____
_____
_____
_____

Mouthfeel:
_____
_____
_____
_____

😋 FLAVOR WHEEL

Earthy — Sharp/Tangy — Buttery/Creamy — Herbal — Salty — Nutty — Toasty — Caramel — Moldy/Blue — Grassy — Robust — Sour — Bitter — Fruity — Milky/Lactic — Sweet

👍 RATING ☆☆☆☆☆

🍷 COMBINED WITH

💬 COMMENTS/SUGGESTIONS

CHEESE Tasting

NAME	
CREAMERY	AGE
RIND	DATE
ORIGIN	PRICE

🥛 MILK

- ☐ Cow
- ☐ Sheep
- ☐ Goat
- ☐ Buffalo
- ☐ Raw
- ☐ _____

🧀 SMELL & TEXTURE

- ☐ Strong
- ☐ Runny
- ☐ Firm
- ☐ Medium
- ☐ Soft
- ☐ Hard
- ☐ Slight
- ☐ Semi-soft
- ☐ Odorless
- ☐ Semi-firm

📝 NOTES

Appearance:
_____
_____
_____
_____

Aroma:
_____
_____
_____

Taste:
_____
_____
_____
_____

Mouthfeel:
_____
_____
_____

😋 FLAVOR WHEEL

Earthy — Sharp/Tangy — Buttery/Creamy — Herbal — Salty — Nutty — Toasty — Caramel — Moldy/Blue — Grassy — Robust — Sour — Bitter — Fruity — Milky/Lactic — Sweet

👍 RATING ☆☆☆☆☆

🍷 COMBINED WITH

💬 COMMENTS/SUGGESTIONS

CHEESE *Tasting*

NAME	
CREAMERY	AGE
RIND	DATE
ORIGIN	PRICE

🥛 MILK

- ☐ Cow
- ☐ Sheep
- ☐ Goat
- ☐ Buffalo
- ☐ Raw
- ☐ _____

🧀 SMELL & TEXTURE

- ☐ Strong
- ☐ Runny
- ☐ Firm
- ☐ Medium
- ☐ Soft
- ☐ Hard
- ☐ Slight
- ☐ Semi-soft
- ☐ Odorless
- ☐ Semi-firm

📝 NOTES

Appearance:

_____
_____
_____

Aroma:

_____
_____
_____

Taste:

_____
_____
_____

Mouthfeel:

_____
_____
_____

😊 FLAVOR WHEEL

Earthy
Sharp/Tangy
Sweet
Buttery/Creamy
Milky/Lactic
Herbal
Fruity
Salty
Bitter
Nutty
Sour
Toasty
Robust
Caramel
Grassy
Moldy/Blue

👍 RATING | ☆ ☆ ☆ ☆ ☆

💬 COMMENTS/SUGGESTIONS

_____
_____
_____
_____
_____
_____
_____
_____
_____
_____
_____
_____
_____

🍷 COMBINED WITH

CHEESE
Tasting

NAME		
CREAMERY		AGE
RIND		DATE
ORIGIN		PRICE

🥛 MILK

☐ Cow   ☐ Sheep

☐ Goat   ☐ Buffalo

☐ Raw   ☐ _____

🧀 SMELL & TEXTURE

☐ Strong   ☐ Runny   ☐ Firm

☐ Medium   ☐ Soft   ☐ Hard

☐ Slight   ☐ Semi-soft

☐ Odorless   ☐ Semi-firm

📝 NOTES

Appearance:

_____

_____

_____

Aroma:

_____

_____

_____

Taste:

_____

_____

_____

Mouthfeel:

_____

_____

_____

😋 FLAVOR WHEEL

Earthy — Sharp/Tangy — Buttery/Creamy — Herbal — Salty — Nutty — Toasty — Caramel — Moldy/Blue — Grassy — Robust — Sour — Bitter — Fruity — Milky/Lactic — Sweet

💬 COMMENTS/SUGGESTIONS

_____

_____

_____

_____

_____

_____

_____

_____

_____

_____

_____

_____

_____

👍 RATING ☆☆☆☆☆

🍷 COMBINED WITH

CHEESE Tasting

NAME	
CREAMERY	AGE
RIND	DATE
ORIGIN	PRICE

🥛 MILK

- ☐ Cow
- ☐ Sheep
- ☐ Goat
- ☐ Buffalo
- ☐ Raw
- ☐ _____

🧀 SMELL & TEXTURE

- ☐ Strong
- ☐ Runny
- ☐ Firm
- ☐ Medium
- ☐ Soft
- ☐ Hard
- ☐ Slight
- ☐ Semi-soft
- ☐ Odorless
- ☐ Semi-firm

📝 NOTES

Appearance:

_____

_____

_____

Aroma:

_____

_____

_____

Taste:

_____

_____

_____

Mouthfeel:

_____

_____

_____

☺ FLAVOR WHEEL

Earthy — Sharp/Tangy — Buttery/Creamy — Herbal — Salty — Nutty — Toasty — Caramel — Moldy/Blue — Grassy — Robust — Sour — Bitter — Fruity — Milky/Lactic — Sweet

👍 RATING | ☆☆☆☆☆

🍷 COMBINED WITH

💬 COMMENTS/SUGGESTIONS

_____

_____

_____

_____

_____

_____

_____

_____

_____

_____

_____

_____

CHEESE Tasting

NAME	
CREAMERY	AGE
RIND	DATE
ORIGIN	PRICE

🥛 MILK

☐ Cow   ☐ Sheep

☐ Goat   ☐ Buffalo

☐ Raw   ☐ _____

🧀 SMELL & TEXTURE

☐ Strong   ☐ Runny   ☐ Firm

☐ Medium   ☐ Soft   ☐ Hard

☐ Slight   ☐ Semi-soft

☐ Odorless   ☐ Semi-firm

📝 NOTES

Appearance:
_____
_____
_____

Aroma:
_____
_____
_____

Taste:
_____
_____
_____

Mouthfeel:
_____
_____
_____

😋 FLAVOR WHEEL

Earthy — Sharp/Tangy — Buttery/Creamy — Herbal — Salty — Nutty — Toasty — Caramel — Moldy/Blue — Grassy — Robust — Sour — Bitter — Fruity — Milky/Lactic — Sweet

⭐ RATING ☆☆☆☆☆

🍷 COMBINED WITH

💬 COMMENTS/SUGGESTIONS

_____
_____
_____
_____
_____
_____
_____
_____
_____
_____
_____
_____

10

CHEESE Tasting

NAME	
CREAMERY	AGE
RIND	DATE
ORIGIN	PRICE

🥛 MILK

- ☐ Cow
- ☐ Sheep
- ☐ Goat
- ☐ Buffalo
- ☐ Raw
- ☐ _____

🧀 SMELL & TEXTURE

- ☐ Strong
- ☐ Medium
- ☐ Slight
- ☐ Odorless
- ☐ Runny
- ☐ Soft
- ☐ Semi-soft
- ☐ Semi-firm
- ☐ Firm
- ☐ Hard

📝 NOTES

Appearance:
_____
_____
_____

Aroma:
_____
_____
_____

Taste:
_____
_____
_____

Mouthfeel:
_____
_____
_____

😋 FLAVOR WHEEL

Earthy — Sharp/Tangy — Buttery/Creamy — Herbal — Salty — Nutty — Toasty — Caramel — Moldy/Blue — Grassy — Robust — Sour — Bitter — Fruity — Milky/Lactic — Sweet

👍 RATING ☆☆☆☆☆

🍷 COMBINED WITH

💬 COMMENTS/SUGGESTIONS
_____
_____
_____
_____
_____
_____
_____
_____
_____
_____
_____
_____

CHEESE Tasting

NAME

CREAMERY	AGE
RIND	DATE
ORIGIN	PRICE

🥛 MILK

- [ ] Cow
- [ ] Goat
- [ ] Raw
- [ ] Sheep
- [ ] Buffalo
- [ ] _____

🧀 SMELL & TEXTURE

- [ ] Strong
- [ ] Medium
- [ ] Slight
- [ ] Odorless
- [ ] Runny
- [ ] Soft
- [ ] Semi-soft
- [ ] Semi-firm
- [ ] Firm
- [ ] Hard

📝 NOTES

Appearance:
_____
_____
_____

Aroma:
_____
_____
_____

Taste:
_____
_____
_____

Mouthfeel:
_____
_____
_____

😋 FLAVOR WHEEL

Earthy — Sharp/Tangy — Buttery/Creamy — Herbal — Salty — Nutty — Toasty — Caramel — Moldy/Blue — Grassy — Robust — Sour — Bitter — Fruity — Milky/Lactic — Sweet

👍 RATING | ☆☆☆☆☆

🍷 COMBINED WITH

💬 COMMENTS/SUGGESTIONS

CHEESE
Tasting

NAME

CREAMERY	AGE
RIND	DATE
ORIGIN	PRICE

🥛 MILK

- ☐ Cow
- ☐ Sheep
- ☐ Goat
- ☐ Buffalo
- ☐ Raw
- ☐ _____

🧀 SMELL & TEXTURE

- ☐ Strong
- ☐ Runny
- ☐ Firm
- ☐ Medium
- ☐ Soft
- ☐ Hard
- ☐ Slight
- ☐ Semi-soft
- ☐ Odorless
- ☐ Semi-firm

📝 NOTES

Appearance: _____
_____
_____
_____

Aroma: _____
_____
_____
_____

Taste: _____
_____
_____
_____

Mouthfeel: _____
_____
_____
_____

😊 FLAVOR WHEEL

Earthy · Sharp/Tangy · Buttery/Creamy · Herbal · Salty · Nutty · Toasty · Caramel · Moldy/Blue · Grassy · Robust · Sour · Bitter · Fruity · Milky/Lactic · Sweet

💬 COMMENTS/SUGGESTIONS

_____
_____
_____
_____
_____
_____
_____
_____
_____
_____
_____
_____

👍 RATING | ☆ ☆ ☆ ☆ ☆

🍷 COMBINED WITH

CHEESE Tasting

NAME		
CREAMERY		AGE
RIND		DATE
ORIGIN		PRICE

🥛 MILK

- ☐ Cow
- ☐ Sheep
- ☐ Goat
- ☐ Buffalo
- ☐ Raw
- ☐ _____

🧀 SMELL & TEXTURE

- ☐ Strong
- ☐ Medium
- ☐ Slight
- ☐ Odorless
- ☐ Runny
- ☐ Soft
- ☐ Semi-soft
- ☐ Semi-firm
- ☐ Firm
- ☐ Hard

📝 NOTES

Appearance:
_____
_____
_____

Aroma:
_____
_____
_____

Taste:
_____
_____
_____

Mouthfeel:
_____
_____
_____

😋 FLAVOR WHEEL

Earthy · Sharp/Tangy · Buttery/Creamy · Herbal · Salty · Nutty · Toasty · Caramel · Moldy/Blue · Grassy · Robust · Sour · Bitter · Fruity · Milky/Lactic · Sweet

👍 RATING ☆☆☆☆☆

🍷 COMBINED WITH

💬 COMMENTS/SUGGESTIONS
_____
_____
_____
_____
_____
_____
_____
_____
_____
_____
_____

14

CHEESE
Tasting

NAME	
CREAMERY	AGE
RIND	DATE
ORIGIN	PRICE

🥛 MILK

☐ Cow ☐ Sheep
☐ Goat ☐ Buffalo
☐ Raw ☐ _____

🧀 SMELL & TEXTURE

☐ Strong ☐ Runny ☐ Firm
☐ Medium ☐ Soft ☐ Hard
☐ Slight ☐ Semi-soft
☐ Odorless ☐ Semi-firm

✍️ NOTES

Appearance:
_____
_____
_____

Aroma:
_____
_____
_____

Taste:
_____
_____
_____

Mouthfeel:
_____
_____
_____

😋 FLAVOR WHEEL

Earthy — Sharp/Tangy
Sweet — Buttery/Creamy
Milky/Lactic — Herbal
Fruity — Salty
Bitter — Nutty
Sour — Toasty
Robust — Caramel
Grassy — Moldy/Blue

💬 COMMENTS/SUGGESTIONS

_____
_____
_____
_____
_____
_____
_____
_____
_____
_____
_____

⭐ RATING ☆☆☆☆☆

🍷 COMBINED WITH

CHEESE Tasting

NAME

CREAMERY	AGE
RIND	DATE
ORIGIN	PRICE

🥛 MILK

- ☐ Cow
- ☐ Sheep
- ☐ Goat
- ☐ Buffalo
- ☐ Raw
- ☐ _____

🧀 SMELL & TEXTURE

- ☐ Strong
- ☐ Runny
- ☐ Firm
- ☐ Medium
- ☐ Soft
- ☐ Hard
- ☐ Slight
- ☐ Semi-soft
- ☐ Odorless
- ☐ Semi-firm

📝 NOTES

Appearance:
_____
_____
_____

Aroma:
_____
_____
_____

Taste:
_____
_____
_____

Mouthfeel:
_____
_____
_____

😊 FLAVOR WHEEL

Earthy · Sharp/Tangy · Buttery/Creamy · Herbal · Salty · Nutty · Toasty · Caramel · Moldy/Blue · Grassy · Robust · Sour · Bitter · Fruity · Milky/Lactic · Sweet

👍 RATING ☆☆☆☆☆

🍷 COMBINED WITH

💬 COMMENTS/SUGGESTIONS

_____
_____
_____
_____
_____
_____
_____
_____
_____
_____
_____
_____

CHEESE Tasting

NAME	
CREAMERY	AGE
RIND	DATE
ORIGIN	PRICE

🥛 MILK

- ☐ Cow
- ☐ Sheep
- ☐ Goat
- ☐ Buffalo
- ☐ Raw
- ☐ _____

🧀 SMELL & TEXTURE

- ☐ Strong
- ☐ Runny
- ☐ Firm
- ☐ Medium
- ☐ Soft
- ☐ Hard
- ☐ Slight
- ☐ Semi-soft
- ☐ Odorless
- ☐ Semi-firm

✍️ NOTES

Appearance: _____
_____
_____
_____

Aroma: _____
_____
_____
_____

Taste: _____
_____
_____
_____

Mouthfeel: _____
_____
_____
_____

😊 FLAVOR WHEEL

Earthy — Sharp/Tangy — Buttery/Creamy — Herbal — Salty — Nutty — Toasty — Caramel — Moldy/Blue — Grassy — Robust — Sour — Bitter — Fruity — Milky/Lactic — Sweet

🔥 RATING ☆☆☆☆☆

🍷 COMBINED WITH

💬 COMMENTS/SUGGESTIONS

_____
_____
_____
_____
_____
_____
_____
_____
_____
_____
_____
_____

CHEESE Tasting

NAME

CREAMERY	AGE
RIND	DATE
ORIGIN	PRICE

🥛 MILK

- ☐ Cow
- ☐ Sheep
- ☐ Goat
- ☐ Buffalo
- ☐ Raw
- ☐ _____

🧀 SMELL & TEXTURE

- ☐ Strong
- ☐ Medium
- ☐ Slight
- ☐ Odorless

- ☐ Runny
- ☐ Soft
- ☐ Semi-soft
- ☐ Semi-firm

- ☐ Firm
- ☐ Hard

📝 NOTES

Appearance:
_____
_____
_____

Aroma:
_____
_____
_____

Taste:
_____
_____
_____

Mouthfeel:
_____
_____
_____

😋 FLAVOR WHEEL

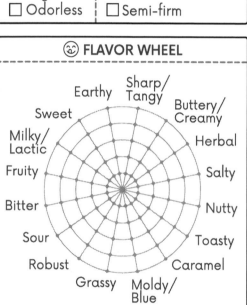

Earthy, Sharp/Tangy, Buttery/Creamy, Sweet, Herbal, Milky/Lactic, Fruity, Salty, Bitter, Nutty, Sour, Toasty, Robust, Caramel, Grassy, Moldy/Blue

👍 RATING | ☆☆☆☆☆

🍷 COMBINED WITH

💬 COMMENTS/SUGGESTIONS

_____
_____
_____
_____
_____
_____
_____
_____
_____
_____
_____

CHEESE Tasting

NAME

CREAMERY | **AGE**

RIND | **DATE**

ORIGIN | **PRICE**

🥛 MILK

- ☐ Cow
- ☐ Goat
- ☐ Raw
- ☐ Sheep
- ☐ Buffalo
- ☐ _____

🧀 SMELL & TEXTURE

- ☐ Strong
- ☐ Medium
- ☐ Slight
- ☐ Odorless
- ☐ Runny
- ☐ Soft
- ☐ Semi-soft
- ☐ Semi-firm
- ☐ Firm
- ☐ Hard

📝 NOTES

Appearance:

_____
_____
_____

Aroma:

_____
_____
_____

Taste:

_____
_____
_____

Mouthfeel:

_____
_____
_____

😋 FLAVOR WHEEL

Earthy — Sharp/Tangy — Buttery/Creamy — Herbal — Salty — Nutty — Toasty — Caramel — Moldy/Blue — Grassy — Robust — Sour — Bitter — Fruity — Milky/Lactic — Sweet

💬 COMMENTS/SUGGESTIONS

_____
_____
_____
_____
_____
_____
_____
_____
_____
_____
_____
_____

🧀 RATING ☆ ☆ ☆ ☆ ☆

🍷 COMBINED WITH

CHEESE Tasting

NAME	
CREAMERY	AGE
RIND	DATE
ORIGIN	PRICE

🥛 MILK

- ☐ Cow
- ☐ Sheep
- ☐ Goat
- ☐ Buffalo
- ☐ Raw
- ☐ _____

🧀 SMELL & TEXTURE

- ☐ Strong
- ☐ Runny
- ☐ Firm
- ☐ Medium
- ☐ Soft
- ☐ Hard
- ☐ Slight
- ☐ Semi-soft
- ☐ Odorless
- ☐ Semi-firm

📝 NOTES

Appearance:
_____
_____
_____

Aroma:
_____
_____
_____

Taste:
_____
_____
_____

Mouthfeel:
_____
_____
_____

😋 FLAVOR WHEEL

Earthy, Sharp/Tangy, Buttery/Creamy, Herbal, Salty, Nutty, Toasty, Caramel, Moldy/Blue, Grassy, Robust, Sour, Bitter, Fruity, Milky/Lactic, Sweet

💬 COMMENTS/SUGGESTIONS

_____
_____
_____
_____
_____
_____
_____
_____
_____
_____
_____
_____
_____
_____

👍 RATING | ☆☆☆☆☆

🍷 COMBINED WITH

CHEESE
tasting

NAME	
CREAMERY	AGE
RIND	DATE
ORIGIN	PRICE

🥛 MILK

- ☐ Cow
- ☐ Sheep
- ☐ Goat
- ☐ Buffalo
- ☐ Raw
- ☐ _____

🧀 SMELL & TEXTURE

- ☐ Strong
- ☐ Medium
- ☐ Slight
- ☐ Odorless
- ☐ Runny
- ☐ Soft
- ☐ Semi-soft
- ☐ Semi-firm
- ☐ Firm
- ☐ Hard

📝 NOTES

Appearance: _____
_____
_____
_____

Aroma: _____
_____
_____
_____

Taste: _____
_____
_____
_____

Mouthfeel: _____
_____
_____
_____

😋 FLAVOR WHEEL

Earthy, Sharp/Tangy, Buttery/Creamy, Sweet, Milky/Lactic, Herbal, Fruity, Salty, Bitter, Nutty, Sour, Toasty, Robust, Caramel, Grassy, Moldy/Blue

⭐ RATING ☆☆☆☆☆

🍷 COMBINED WITH

💬 COMMENTS/SUGGESTIONS

CHEESE Tasting

NAME		
CREAMERY	AGE	
RIND	DATE	
ORIGIN	PRICE	

🥛 MILK

- ☐ Cow
- ☐ Sheep
- ☐ Goat
- ☐ Buffalo
- ☐ Raw
- ☐ _____

🧀 SMELL & TEXTURE

- ☐ Strong
- ☐ Runny
- ☐ Firm
- ☐ Medium
- ☐ Soft
- ☐ Hard
- ☐ Slight
- ☐ Semi-soft
- ☐ Odorless
- ☐ Semi-firm

📝 NOTES

Appearance:
_____
_____
_____

Aroma:
_____
_____
_____

Taste:
_____
_____
_____

Mouthfeel:
_____
_____
_____

😀 FLAVOR WHEEL

Earthy · Sharp/Tangy · Buttery/Creamy · Herbal · Sweet · Milky/Lactic · Fruity · Salty · Bitter · Nutty · Sour · Toasty · Robust · Caramel · Grassy · Moldy/Blue

⭐ RATING ☆☆☆☆☆

🍷 COMBINED WITH

💬 COMMENTS/SUGGESTIONS

_____
_____
_____
_____
_____
_____
_____
_____
_____
_____

22

CHEESE
Tasting

NAME

CREAMERY	AGE
RIND	DATE
ORIGIN	PRICE

🥛 MILK

- ☐ Cow
- ☐ Sheep
- ☐ Goat
- ☐ Buffalo
- ☐ Raw
- ☐ _____

🧀 SMELL & TEXTURE

- ☐ Strong
- ☐ Medium
- ☐ Slight
- ☐ Odorless
- ☐ Runny
- ☐ Soft
- ☐ Semi-soft
- ☐ Semi-firm
- ☐ Firm
- ☐ Hard

📝 NOTES

Appearance: _____
_____
_____
_____

Aroma: _____
_____
_____
_____

Taste: _____
_____
_____
_____

Mouthfeel: _____
_____
_____
_____

😋 FLAVOR WHEEL

Earthy · Sharp/Tangy · Buttery/Creamy · Sweet · Herbal · Milky/Lactic · Fruity · Salty · Bitter · Nutty · Sour · Toasty · Robust · Caramel · Grassy · Moldy/Blue

👍 RATING ☆☆☆☆☆

🍷 COMBINED WITH

💬 COMMENTS/SUGGESTIONS

CHEESE Tasting

NAME	
CREAMERY	AGE
RIND	DATE
ORIGIN	PRICE

🥛 MILK

- ☐ Cow
- ☐ Sheep
- ☐ Goat
- ☐ Buffalo
- ☐ Raw
- ☐ _____

🧀 SMELL & TEXTURE

- ☐ Strong
- ☐ Runny
- ☐ Firm
- ☐ Medium
- ☐ Soft
- ☐ Hard
- ☐ Slight
- ☐ Semi-soft
- ☐ Odorless
- ☐ Semi-firm

✍️ NOTES

Appearance:
_____
_____
_____

Aroma:
_____
_____
_____

Taste:
_____
_____
_____
_____

Mouthfeel:
_____
_____
_____

😋 FLAVOR WHEEL

Earthy
Sharp/Tangy
Sweet
Buttery/Creamy
Milky/Lactic
Herbal
Fruity
Salty
Bitter
Nutty
Sour
Toasty
Robust
Caramel
Grassy
Moldy/Blue

👍 RATING | ☆☆☆☆☆

🍷 COMBINED WITH

💬 COMMENTS/SUGGESTIONS

_____
_____
_____
_____
_____
_____
_____
_____
_____
_____
_____
_____
_____

CHEESE
Tasting

NAME

CREAMERY | AGE

RIND | DATE

ORIGIN | PRICE

🥛 MILK

- ☐ Cow
- ☐ Sheep
- ☐ Goat
- ☐ Buffalo
- ☐ Raw
- ☐ _____

🧀 SMELL & TEXTURE

- ☐ Strong
- ☐ Medium
- ☐ Slight
- ☐ Odorless
- ☐ Runny
- ☐ Soft
- ☐ Semi-soft
- ☐ Semi-firm
- ☐ Firm
- ☐ Hard

📝 NOTES

Appearance:
_____
_____
_____

Aroma:
_____
_____
_____

Taste:
_____
_____
_____
_____

Mouthfeel:
_____
_____
_____

😋 FLAVOR WHEEL

Earthy · Sharp/Tangy · Buttery/Creamy · Herbal · Salty · Nutty · Toasty · Caramel · Moldy/Blue · Grassy · Robust · Sour · Bitter · Fruity · Milky/Lactic · Sweet

👍 RATING | ☆☆☆☆☆

🍷 COMBINED WITH

💬 COMMENTS/SUGGESTIONS

CHEESE Tasting

NAME	
CREAMERY	AGE
RIND	DATE
ORIGIN	PRICE

🥛 MILK

- ☐ Cow
- ☐ Sheep
- ☐ Goat
- ☐ Buffalo
- ☐ Raw
- ☐ _____

🧀 SMELL & TEXTURE

- ☐ Strong
- ☐ Runny
- ☐ Firm
- ☐ Medium
- ☐ Soft
- ☐ Hard
- ☐ Slight
- ☐ Semi-soft
- ☐ Odorless
- ☐ Semi-firm

📝 NOTES

Appearance:

_____

_____

_____

Aroma:

_____

_____

_____

Taste:

_____

_____

_____

Mouthfeel:

_____

_____

_____

😋 FLAVOR WHEEL

Earthy, Sharp/Tangy, Buttery/Creamy, Sweet, Herbal, Milky/Lactic, Fruity, Salty, Bitter, Nutty, Sour, Toasty, Robust, Caramel, Grassy, Moldy/Blue

👍 RATING ☆☆☆☆☆

🍷 COMBINED WITH

💬 COMMENTS/SUGGESTIONS

CHEESE *Tasting*

NAME	
CREAMERY	AGE
RIND	DATE
ORIGIN	PRICE

🥛 MILK

- ☐ Cow
- ☐ Sheep
- ☐ Goat
- ☐ Buffalo
- ☐ Raw
- ☐ _____

🧀 SMELL & TEXTURE

- ☐ Strong
- ☐ Medium
- ☐ Slight
- ☐ Odorless
- ☐ Runny
- ☐ Soft
- ☐ Semi-soft
- ☐ Semi-firm
- ☐ Firm
- ☐ Hard

📝 NOTES

Appearance:

_____
_____
_____

Aroma:

_____
_____
_____

Taste:

_____
_____
_____

Mouthfeel:

_____
_____
_____

😋 FLAVOR WHEEL

Earthy
Sharp/Tangy
Buttery/Creamy
Sweet
Herbal
Milky/Lactic
Fruity
Salty
Bitter
Nutty
Sour
Toasty
Robust
Caramel
Grassy
Moldy/Blue

👍 RATING | ☆☆☆☆☆

🍷 COMBINED WITH

💬 COMMENTS/SUGGESTIONS

CHEESE
Tasting

NAME	
CREAMERY	AGE
RIND	DATE
ORIGIN	PRICE

🥛 MILK

- ☐ Cow
- ☐ Sheep
- ☐ Goat
- ☐ Buffalo
- ☐ Raw
- ☐ _____

🧀 SMELL & TEXTURE

- ☐ Strong
- ☐ Runny
- ☐ Firm
- ☐ Medium
- ☐ Soft
- ☐ Hard
- ☐ Slight
- ☐ Semi-soft
- ☐ Odorless
- ☐ Semi-firm

📝 NOTES

Appearance:
_____
_____
_____
_____

Aroma:
_____
_____
_____
_____

Taste:
_____
_____
_____
_____

Mouthfeel:
_____
_____
_____
_____

😊 FLAVOR WHEEL

Earthy — Sharp/Tangy — Buttery/Creamy — Herbal — Salty — Nutty — Toasty — Caramel — Moldy/Blue — Grassy — Robust — Sour — Bitter — Fruity — Milky/Lactic — Sweet

💬 COMMENTS/SUGGESTIONS

_____
_____
_____
_____
_____
_____
_____
_____
_____
_____
_____
_____
_____

👍 RATING | ☆ ☆ ☆ ☆ ☆

🍷 COMBINED WITH

CHEESE Tasting

NAME		
CREAMERY	**AGE**	
RIND	**DATE**	
ORIGIN	**PRICE**	

🥛 MILK

☐ Cow ☐ Sheep
☐ Goat ☐ Buffalo
☐ Raw ☐ _____

🧀 SMELL & TEXTURE

☐ Strong ☐ Runny ☐ Firm
☐ Medium ☐ Soft ☐ Hard
☐ Slight ☐ Semi-soft
☐ Odorless ☐ Semi-firm

📝 NOTES

Appearance: _____
_____
_____
_____

Aroma: _____
_____
_____
_____

Taste: _____
_____
_____
_____

Mouthfeel: _____
_____
_____
_____

😋 FLAVOR WHEEL

Earthy, Sharp/Tangy, Buttery/Creamy, Herbal, Salty, Nutty, Toasty, Caramel, Moldy/Blue, Grassy, Robust, Sour, Bitter, Fruity, Milky/Lactic, Sweet

💬 COMMENTS/SUGGESTIONS

🧀 RATING ☆ ☆ ☆ ☆ ☆

🍷 COMBINED WITH

CHEESE
Tasting

NAME		
CREAMERY		AGE
RIND		DATE
ORIGIN		PRICE

🥛 MILK

- ☐ Cow
- ☐ Sheep
- ☐ Goat
- ☐ Buffalo
- ☐ Raw
- ☐ _____

🧀 SMELL & TEXTURE

- ☐ Strong
- ☐ Medium
- ☐ Slight
- ☐ Odorless
- ☐ Runny
- ☐ Soft
- ☐ Semi-soft
- ☐ Semi-firm
- ☐ Firm
- ☐ Hard

📝 NOTES

Appearance:

_____
_____
_____

Aroma:

_____
_____
_____

Taste:

_____
_____
_____

Mouthfeel:

_____
_____
_____

😋 FLAVOR WHEEL

Earthy · Sharp/Tangy · Buttery/Creamy · Herbal · Sweet · Milky/Lactic · Fruity · Salty · Bitter · Nutty · Sour · Toasty · Robust · Caramel · Grassy · Moldy/Blue

💬 COMMENTS/SUGGESTIONS

_____
_____
_____
_____
_____
_____
_____
_____
_____
_____
_____
_____
_____

👍 RATING | ☆☆☆☆☆

🍷 COMBINED WITH

CHEESE
Tasting

NAME		
CREAMERY		AGE
RIND		DATE
ORIGIN		PRICE

🥛 MILK

- ☐ Cow
- ☐ Sheep
- ☐ Goat
- ☐ Buffalo
- ☐ Raw
- ☐ _____

🧀 SMELL & TEXTURE

- ☐ Strong
- ☐ Medium
- ☐ Slight
- ☐ Odorless
- ☐ Runny
- ☐ Soft
- ☐ Semi-soft
- ☐ Semi-firm
- ☐ Firm
- ☐ Hard

📝 NOTES

Appearance:
_____
_____
_____

Aroma:
_____
_____
_____

Taste:
_____
_____
_____
_____

Mouthfeel:
_____
_____
_____

😋 FLAVOR WHEEL

Earthy · Sharp/Tangy · Buttery/Creamy · Sweet · Herbal · Milky/Lactic · Fruity · Salty · Bitter · Nutty · Sour · Toasty · Robust · Caramel · Grassy · Moldy/Blue

👍 RATING ☆☆☆☆☆

🍷 COMBINED WITH

💬 COMMENTS/SUGGESTIONS

CHEESE Tasting

NAME	
CREAMERY	AGE
RIND	DATE
ORIGIN	PRICE

🥛 MILK

- ☐ Cow
- ☐ Sheep
- ☐ Goat
- ☐ Buffalo
- ☐ Raw
- ☐ _____

🧀 SMELL & TEXTURE

- ☐ Strong
- ☐ Runny
- ☐ Firm
- ☐ Medium
- ☐ Soft
- ☐ Hard
- ☐ Slight
- ☐ Semi-soft
- ☐ Odorless
- ☐ Semi-firm

📝 NOTES

Appearance:
_____
_____
_____
_____

Aroma:
_____
_____
_____

Taste:
_____
_____
_____
_____

Mouthfeel:
_____
_____
_____

😋 FLAVOR WHEEL

Earthy, Sharp/Tangy, Buttery/Creamy, Sweet, Herbal, Milky/Lactic, Fruity, Salty, Bitter, Nutty, Sour, Toasty, Robust, Caramel, Grassy, Moldy/Blue

🖐 RATING ☆☆☆☆☆

🍷 COMBINED WITH

💬 COMMENTS/SUGGESTIONS

_____
_____
_____
_____
_____
_____
_____
_____
_____
_____
_____
_____

CHEESE Tasting

NAME		
CREAMERY		AGE
RIND		DATE
ORIGIN		PRICE

🥛 MILK

- ☐ Cow
- ☐ Sheep
- ☐ Goat
- ☐ Buffalo
- ☐ Raw
- ☐ _____

🧀 SMELL & TEXTURE

- ☐ Strong
- ☐ Medium
- ☐ Slight
- ☐ Odorless

- ☐ Runny
- ☐ Soft
- ☐ Semi-soft
- ☐ Semi-firm

- ☐ Firm
- ☐ Hard

📝 NOTES

Appearance: _____
_____
_____
_____

Aroma: _____
_____
_____
_____

Taste: _____
_____
_____
_____

Mouthfeel: _____
_____
_____
_____

😋 FLAVOR WHEEL

Earthy / Sharp/Tangy / Buttery/Creamy / Sweet / Herbal / Milky/Lactic / Fruity / Salty / Bitter / Nutty / Sour / Toasty / Robust / Caramel / Grassy / Moldy/Blue

👍 RATING ☆☆☆☆☆

🍷 COMBINED WITH

💬 COMMENTS/SUGGESTIONS

33

CHEESE Tasting

NAME	
CREAMERY	AGE
RIND	DATE
ORIGIN	PRICE

🥛 MILK

- ☐ Cow
- ☐ Sheep
- ☐ Goat
- ☐ Buffalo
- ☐ Raw
- ☐ _____

🧀 SMELL & TEXTURE

- ☐ Strong
- ☐ Runny
- ☐ Firm
- ☐ Medium
- ☐ Soft
- ☐ Hard
- ☐ Slight
- ☐ Semi-soft
- ☐ Odorless
- ☐ Semi-firm

📝 NOTES

Appearance:
_____
_____
_____

Aroma:
_____
_____
_____

Taste:
_____
_____
_____

Mouthfeel:
_____
_____
_____

😋 FLAVOR WHEEL

Earthy
Sharp/Tangy
Sweet
Buttery/Creamy
Milky/Lactic
Herbal
Fruity
Salty
Bitter
Nutty
Sour
Toasty
Robust
Caramel
Grassy
Moldy/Blue

💬 COMMENTS/SUGGESTIONS

_____
_____
_____
_____
_____
_____
_____
_____
_____
_____
_____
_____

👍 RATING ☆ ☆ ☆ ☆ ☆

🍷 COMBINED WITH

CHEESE Tasting

NAME		
CREAMERY		AGE
RIND		DATE
ORIGIN		PRICE

🥛 MILK

- ☐ Cow
- ☐ Sheep
- ☐ Goat
- ☐ Buffalo
- ☐ Raw
- ☐ _____

🧀 SMELL & TEXTURE

- ☐ Strong
- ☐ Runny
- ☐ Firm
- ☐ Medium
- ☐ Soft
- ☐ Hard
- ☐ Slight
- ☐ Semi-soft
- ☐ Odorless
- ☐ Semi-firm

📝 NOTES

Appearance: _____
_____
_____
_____

Aroma: _____
_____
_____
_____

Taste: _____
_____
_____
_____

Mouthfeel: _____
_____
_____
_____

😋 FLAVOR WHEEL

Earthy
Sharp/Tangy
Sweet
Buttery/Creamy
Milky/Lactic
Herbal
Fruity
Salty
Bitter
Nutty
Sour
Toasty
Robust
Caramel
Grassy
Moldy/Blue

💬 COMMENTS/SUGGESTIONS

⭐ RATING | ☆☆☆☆☆

🍷 COMBINED WITH

CHEESE Tasting

NAME	
CREAMERY	AGE
RIND	DATE
ORIGIN	PRICE

🥛 MILK

- ☐ Cow
- ☐ Sheep
- ☐ Goat
- ☐ Buffalo
- ☐ Raw
- ☐ _____

🧀 SMELL & TEXTURE

- ☐ Strong
- ☐ Runny
- ☐ Firm
- ☐ Medium
- ☐ Soft
- ☐ Hard
- ☐ Slight
- ☐ Semi-soft
- ☐ Odorless
- ☐ Semi-firm

📝 NOTES

Appearance: _____
_____
_____
_____

Aroma: _____
_____
_____
_____

Taste: _____
_____
_____
_____

Mouthfeel: _____
_____
_____
_____

😋 FLAVOR WHEEL

Earthy
Sharp/Tangy
Sweet
Buttery/Creamy
Milky/Lactic
Herbal
Fruity
Salty
Bitter
Nutty
Sour
Toasty
Robust
Caramel
Grassy
Moldy/Blue

⭐ RATING ☆☆☆☆☆

🍷 COMBINED WITH

💬 COMMENTS/SUGGESTIONS

CHEESE Tasting

NAME	
CREAMERY	AGE
RIND	DATE
ORIGIN	PRICE

🥛 MILK

- ☐ Cow
- ☐ Sheep
- ☐ Goat
- ☐ Buffalo
- ☐ Raw
- ☐ _____

🧀 SMELL & TEXTURE

- ☐ Strong
- ☐ Medium
- ☐ Slight
- ☐ Odorless
- ☐ Runny
- ☐ Soft
- ☐ Semi-soft
- ☐ Semi-firm
- ☐ Firm
- ☐ Hard

📝 NOTES

Appearance: _____
_____
_____
_____

Aroma: _____
_____
_____
_____

Taste: _____
_____
_____
_____

Mouthfeel: _____
_____
_____
_____

😋 FLAVOR WHEEL

Earthy, Sharp/Tangy, Buttery/Creamy, Herbal, Salty, Nutty, Toasty, Caramel, Moldy/Blue, Grassy, Robust, Sour, Bitter, Fruity, Milky/Lactic, Sweet

⭐ RATING ☆☆☆☆☆

🍷 COMBINED WITH

💬 COMMENTS/SUGGESTIONS

CHEESE Tasting

NAME		
CREAMERY		AGE
RIND		DATE
ORIGIN		PRICE

🥛 MILK

☐ Cow ☐ Sheep
☐ Goat ☐ Buffalo
☐ Raw ☐ _____

🧀 SMELL & TEXTURE

☐ Strong ☐ Runny ☐ Firm
☐ Medium ☐ Soft ☐ Hard
☐ Slight ☐ Semi-soft
☐ Odorless ☐ Semi-firm

📝 NOTES

Appearance:
_____
_____
_____

Aroma:
_____
_____
_____

Taste:
_____
_____
_____

Mouthfeel:
_____
_____
_____

😋 FLAVOR WHEEL

Earthy — Sharp/Tangy — Buttery/Creamy — Herbal — Salty — Nutty — Toasty — Caramel — Moldy/Blue — Grassy — Robust — Sour — Bitter — Fruity — Milky/Lactic — Sweet

💬 COMMENTS/SUGGESTIONS

_____
_____
_____
_____
_____
_____
_____
_____
_____
_____
_____

🧀 RATING ☆☆☆☆☆

🍷 COMBINED WITH

CHEESE
Tasting

NAME

CREAMERY	AGE
RIND	DATE
ORIGIN	PRICE

🥛 MILK

- ☐ Cow
- ☐ Sheep
- ☐ Goat
- ☐ Buffalo
- ☐ Raw
- ☐ _____

🧀 SMELL & TEXTURE

- ☐ Strong
- ☐ Medium
- ☐ Slight
- ☐ Odorless
- ☐ Runny
- ☐ Soft
- ☐ Semi-soft
- ☐ Semi-firm
- ☐ Firm
- ☐ Hard

📝 NOTES

Appearance:
_____
_____
_____

Aroma:
_____
_____
_____

Taste:
_____
_____
_____

Mouthfeel:
_____
_____
_____

😋 FLAVOR WHEEL

Earthy
Sharp/Tangy
Sweet
Buttery/Creamy
Milky/Lactic
Herbal
Fruity
Salty
Bitter
Nutty
Sour
Toasty
Robust
Caramel
Grassy
Moldy/Blue

⭐ RATING ☆☆☆☆☆

🍷 COMBINED WITH

💬 COMMENTS/SUGGESTIONS

CHEESE
Tasting

NAME	
CREAMERY	AGE
RIND	DATE
ORIGIN	PRICE

🥛 MILK

☐ Cow ☐ Sheep
☐ Goat ☐ Buffalo
☐ Raw ☐ _____

🧀 SMELL & TEXTURE

☐ Strong ☐ Runny ☐ Firm
☐ Medium ☐ Soft ☐ Hard
☐ Slight ☐ Semi-soft
☐ Odorless ☐ Semi-firm

📝 NOTES

Appearance:
_____
_____
_____

Aroma:
_____
_____
_____

Taste:
_____
_____
_____

Mouthfeel:
_____
_____
_____

😊 FLAVOR WHEEL

Earthy — Sharp/Tangy — Buttery/Creamy — Herbal — Salty — Nutty — Toasty — Caramel — Moldy/Blue — Grassy — Robust — Sour — Bitter — Fruity — Milky/Lactic — Sweet

😋 COMMENTS/SUGGESTIONS

_____
_____
_____
_____
_____
_____
_____
_____
_____
_____
_____
_____

👍 RATING ☆☆☆☆☆

🍷 COMBINED WITH

CHEESE
Tasting

NAME		
CREAMERY		AGE
RIND		DATE
ORIGIN		PRICE

🥛 MILK

- [ ] Cow
- [ ] Goat
- [ ] Raw
- [ ] Sheep
- [ ] Buffalo
- [ ] _____

🧀 SMELL & TEXTURE

- [ ] Strong
- [ ] Medium
- [ ] Slight
- [ ] Odorless
- [ ] Runny
- [ ] Soft
- [ ] Semi-soft
- [ ] Semi-firm
- [ ] Firm
- [ ] Hard

📝 NOTES

Appearance: _____
_____
_____
_____

Aroma: _____
_____
_____
_____

Taste: _____
_____
_____
_____

Mouthfeel: _____
_____
_____
_____

😋 FLAVOR WHEEL

Earthy
Sharp/Tangy
Buttery/Creamy
Sweet
Herbal
Milky/Lactic
Fruity
Salty
Bitter
Nutty
Sour
Toasty
Robust
Caramel
Grassy
Moldy/Blue

👍 RATING | ☆ ☆ ☆ ☆ ☆

🍷 COMBINED WITH

💬 COMMENTS/SUGGESTIONS

CHEESE Tasting

NAME	
CREAMERY	AGE
RIND	DATE
ORIGIN	PRICE

🥛 MILK

☐ Cow ☐ Sheep
☐ Goat ☐ Buffalo
☐ Raw ☐ _____

🧀 SMELL & TEXTURE

☐ Strong ☐ Runny ☐ Firm
☐ Medium ☐ Soft ☐ Hard
☐ Slight ☐ Semi-soft
☐ Odorless ☐ Semi-firm

📝 NOTES

Appearance:
_____
_____
_____

Aroma:
_____
_____
_____

Taste:
_____
_____
_____

Mouthfeel:
_____
_____
_____

😋 FLAVOR WHEEL

Earthy, Sharp/Tangy, Buttery/Creamy, Sweet, Herbal, Milky/Lactic, Fruity, Salty, Bitter, Nutty, Sour, Toasty, Robust, Caramel, Grassy, Moldy/Blue

👍 RATING | ☆☆☆☆☆

🍷 COMBINED WITH

💬 COMMENTS/SUGGESTIONS

CHEESE
Tasting

NAME		
CREAMERY		AGE
RIND		DATE
ORIGIN		PRICE

🥛 MILK

- ☐ Cow
- ☐ Sheep
- ☐ Goat
- ☐ Buffalo
- ☐ Raw
- ☐ _____

🧀 SMELL & TEXTURE

- ☐ Strong
- ☐ Medium
- ☐ Slight
- ☐ Odorless

- ☐ Runny
- ☐ Soft
- ☐ Semi-soft
- ☐ Semi-firm

- ☐ Firm
- ☐ Hard

📝 NOTES

Appearance:
_____
_____
_____

Aroma:
_____
_____
_____

Taste:
_____
_____
_____

Mouthfeel:
_____
_____
_____

😋 FLAVOR WHEEL

Sharp/Tangy
Earthy
Buttery/Creamy
Sweet
Herbal
Milky/Lactic
Fruity
Salty
Bitter
Nutty
Sour
Toasty
Robust
Caramel
Grassy
Moldy/Blue

💬 COMMENTS/SUGGESTIONS

_____
_____
_____
_____
_____
_____
_____
_____
_____
_____
_____
_____

🧀 RATING ☆☆☆☆☆

🍷 COMBINED WITH

CHEESE Tasting

NAME	
CREAMERY	AGE
RIND	DATE
ORIGIN	PRICE

🥛 MILK

- ☐ Cow
- ☐ Sheep
- ☐ Goat
- ☐ Buffalo
- ☐ Raw
- ☐ _____

🧀 SMELL & TEXTURE

- ☐ Strong
- ☐ Runny
- ☐ Firm
- ☐ Medium
- ☐ Soft
- ☐ Hard
- ☐ Slight
- ☐ Semi-soft
- ☐ Odorless
- ☐ Semi-firm

📝 NOTES

Appearance:
_____
_____
_____

Aroma:
_____
_____
_____

Taste:
_____
_____
_____

Mouthfeel:
_____
_____
_____

😋 FLAVOR WHEEL

Earthy · Sharp/Tangy · Buttery/Creamy · Herbal · Salty · Nutty · Toasty · Caramel · Moldy/Blue · Grassy · Robust · Sour · Bitter · Fruity · Milky/Lactic · Sweet

👍 RATING ☆☆☆☆☆

🍷 COMBINED WITH

💬 COMMENTS/SUGGESTIONS

_____
_____
_____
_____
_____
_____
_____
_____
_____
_____
_____
_____
_____
_____

CHEESE
Tasting

NAME		
CREAMERY		AGE
RIND		DATE
ORIGIN		PRICE

🥛 MILK

- ☐ Cow
- ☐ Sheep
- ☐ Goat
- ☐ Buffalo
- ☐ Raw
- ☐ _____

🧀 SMELL & TEXTURE

- ☐ Strong
- ☐ Runny
- ☐ Firm
- ☐ Medium
- ☐ Soft
- ☐ Hard
- ☐ Slight
- ☐ Semi-soft
- ☐ Odorless
- ☐ Semi-firm

📝 NOTES

Appearance:

_____
_____
_____

Aroma:

_____
_____
_____

Taste:

_____
_____
_____

Mouthfeel:

_____
_____
_____

😋 FLAVOR WHEEL

Earthy
Sharp/Tangy
Sweet
Buttery/Creamy
Milky/Lactic
Herbal
Fruity
Salty
Bitter
Nutty
Sour
Toasty
Robust
Caramel
Grassy
Moldy/Blue

💬 COMMENTS/SUGGESTIONS

🧀 RATING ☆☆☆☆☆

🍷 COMBINED WITH

CHEESE Tasting

NAME	
CREAMERY	AGE
RIND	DATE
ORIGIN	PRICE

🥛 MILK

- ☐ Cow
- ☐ Sheep
- ☐ Goat
- ☐ Buffalo
- ☐ Raw
- ☐ _____

🧀 SMELL & TEXTURE

- ☐ Strong
- ☐ Runny
- ☐ Firm
- ☐ Medium
- ☐ Soft
- ☐ Hard
- ☐ Slight
- ☐ Semi-soft
- ☐ Odorless
- ☐ Semi-firm

📝 NOTES

Appearance:
_____
_____
_____

Aroma:
_____
_____
_____

Taste:
_____
_____
_____

Mouthfeel:
_____
_____
_____

☺ FLAVOR WHEEL

Earthy · Sharp/Tangy · Buttery/Creamy · Herbal · Salty · Nutty · Toasty · Caramel · Moldy/Blue · Grassy · Robust · Sour · Bitter · Fruity · Milky/Lactic · Sweet

🖐 RATING ☆☆☆☆☆

🍷 COMBINED WITH

💬 COMMENTS/SUGGESTIONS

_____
_____
_____
_____
_____
_____
_____
_____
_____
_____
_____
_____
_____

CHEESE
Tasting

NAME

CREAMERY	AGE
RIND	DATE
ORIGIN	PRICE

🥛 MILK

- ☐ Cow
- ☐ Sheep
- ☐ Goat
- ☐ Buffalo
- ☐ Raw
- ☐ _____

🧀 SMELL & TEXTURE

- ☐ Strong
- ☐ Runny
- ☐ Firm
- ☐ Medium
- ☐ Soft
- ☐ Hard
- ☐ Slight
- ☐ Semi-soft
- ☐ Odorless
- ☐ Semi-firm

📝 NOTES

Appearance: _____
_____
_____
_____

Aroma: _____
_____
_____
_____

Taste: _____
_____
_____
_____

Mouthfeel: _____
_____
_____
_____

😋 FLAVOR WHEEL

Earthy — Sharp/Tangy — Buttery/Creamy — Herbal — Salty — Nutty — Toasty — Caramel — Moldy/Blue — Grassy — Robust — Sour — Bitter — Fruity — Milky/Lactic — Sweet

💬 COMMENTS/SUGGESTIONS

👍 RATING ☆ ☆ ☆ ☆ ☆

🍷 COMBINED WITH

CHEESE Tasting

NAME

CREAMERY	AGE
RIND	DATE
ORIGIN	PRICE

🥛 MILK

- ☐ Cow
- ☐ Goat
- ☐ Raw
- ☐ Sheep
- ☐ Buffalo
- ☐ _____

🧀 SMELL & TEXTURE

- ☐ Strong
- ☐ Medium
- ☐ Slight
- ☐ Odorless

- ☐ Runny
- ☐ Soft
- ☐ Semi-soft
- ☐ Semi-firm

- ☐ Firm
- ☐ Hard

📝 NOTES

Appearance:
_____
_____
_____

Aroma:
_____
_____
_____

Taste:
_____
_____
_____

Mouthfeel:
_____
_____
_____

😋 FLAVOR WHEEL

Earthy · Sharp/Tangy · Buttery/Creamy · Herbal · Salty · Nutty · Toasty · Caramel · Moldy/Blue · Grassy · Robust · Sour · Bitter · Fruity · Milky/Lactic · Sweet

⭐ RATING ☆☆☆☆☆

🍷 COMBINED WITH

💬 COMMENTS/SUGGESTIONS
_____
_____
_____
_____
_____
_____
_____
_____
_____
_____
_____

CHEESE Tasting

NAME		
CREAMERY		AGE
RIND		DATE
ORIGIN		PRICE

🥛 MILK

- ☐ Cow
- ☐ Sheep
- ☐ Goat
- ☐ Buffalo
- ☐ Raw
- ☐ _____

🧀 SMELL & TEXTURE

- ☐ Strong
- ☐ Runny
- ☐ Firm
- ☐ Medium
- ☐ Soft
- ☐ Hard
- ☐ Slight
- ☐ Semi-soft
- ☐ Odorless
- ☐ Semi-firm

📝 NOTES

Appearance:
_____
_____
_____

Aroma:
_____
_____
_____

Taste:
_____
_____
_____

Mouthfeel:
_____
_____
_____

😋 FLAVOR WHEEL

Earthy — Sharp/Tangy — Buttery/Creamy — Herbal — Salty — Nutty — Toasty — Caramel — Moldy/Blue — Grassy — Robust — Sour — Bitter — Fruity — Milky/Lactic — Sweet

👍 RATING ☆☆☆☆☆

🍷 COMBINED WITH

💬 COMMENTS/SUGGESTIONS
_____
_____
_____
_____
_____
_____
_____
_____
_____
_____
_____
_____

CHEESE Tasting

NAME	
CREAMERY	AGE
RIND	DATE
ORIGIN	PRICE

🥛 MILK

- ☐ Cow
- ☐ Sheep
- ☐ Goat
- ☐ Buffalo
- ☐ Raw
- ☐ _____

🧀 SMELL & TEXTURE

- ☐ Strong
- ☐ Runny
- ☐ Firm
- ☐ Medium
- ☐ Soft
- ☐ Hard
- ☐ Slight
- ☐ Semi-soft
- ☐ Odorless
- ☐ Semi-firm

📝 NOTES

Appearance:

_____
_____
_____

Aroma:

_____
_____
_____

Taste:

_____
_____
_____

Mouthfeel:

_____
_____
_____

😊 FLAVOR WHEEL

Earthy — Sharp/Tangy — Buttery/Creamy — Herbal — Salty — Nutty — Toasty — Caramel — Moldy/Blue — Grassy — Robust — Sour — Bitter — Fruity — Milky/Lactic — Sweet

👍 RATING ☆☆☆☆☆

🍷 COMBINED WITH

💬 COMMENTS/SUGGESTIONS

_____
_____
_____
_____
_____
_____
_____
_____
_____
_____
_____
_____

CHEESE
Tasting

NAME		
CREAMERY	AGE	
RIND	DATE	
ORIGIN	PRICE	

🥛 MILK

- ☐ Cow
- ☐ Sheep
- ☐ Goat
- ☐ Buffalo
- ☐ Raw
- ☐ _____

🧀 SMELL & TEXTURE

- ☐ Strong
- ☐ Runny
- ☐ Firm
- ☐ Medium
- ☐ Soft
- ☐ Hard
- ☐ Slight
- ☐ Semi-soft
- ☐ Odorless
- ☐ Semi-firm

📝 NOTES

Appearance:
_____
_____
_____

Aroma:
_____
_____
_____

Taste:
_____
_____
_____

Mouthfeel:
_____
_____
_____

😋 FLAVOR WHEEL

Earthy · Sharp/Tangy · Buttery/Creamy · Sweet · Herbal · Milky/Lactic · Fruity · Salty · Bitter · Nutty · Sour · Toasty · Robust · Caramel · Grassy · Moldy/Blue

💬 COMMENTS/SUGGESTIONS

_____
_____
_____
_____
_____
_____
_____
_____
_____
_____
_____
_____

👍 RATING | ☆☆☆☆☆

🍷 COMBINED WITH

CHEESE Tasting

NAME	
CREAMERY	AGE
RIND	DATE
ORIGIN	PRICE

🥛 MILK

- ☐ Cow
- ☐ Sheep
- ☐ Goat
- ☐ Buffalo
- ☐ Raw
- ☐ _____

🧀 SMELL & TEXTURE

- ☐ Strong
- ☐ Runny
- ☐ Firm
- ☐ Medium
- ☐ Soft
- ☐ Hard
- ☐ Slight
- ☐ Semi-soft
- ☐ Odorless
- ☐ Semi-firm

📝 NOTES

Appearance:
_____
_____
_____
_____

Aroma:
_____
_____
_____

Taste:
_____
_____
_____

Mouthfeel:
_____
_____
_____

😋 FLAVOR WHEEL

Earthy
Sharp/Tangy
Sweet
Buttery/Creamy
Milky/Lactic
Herbal
Fruity
Salty
Bitter
Nutty
Sour
Toasty
Robust
Caramel
Grassy
Moldy/Blue

💬 COMMENTS/SUGGESTIONS

_____
_____
_____
_____
_____
_____
_____
_____
_____
_____
_____
_____

👍 RATING | ☆☆☆☆☆

🍷 COMBINED WITH

52

CHEESE *Tasting*

NAME		
CREAMERY		AGE
RIND		DATE
ORIGIN		PRICE

🥛 MILK

- ☐ Cow
- ☐ Sheep
- ☐ Goat
- ☐ Buffalo
- ☐ Raw
- ☐ _____

🧀 SMELL & TEXTURE

- ☐ Strong
- ☐ Medium
- ☐ Slight
- ☐ Odorless
- ☐ Runny
- ☐ Soft
- ☐ Semi-soft
- ☐ Semi-firm
- ☐ Firm
- ☐ Hard

📝 NOTES

Appearance:

Aroma:

Taste:

Mouthfeel:

😋 FLAVOR WHEEL

Earthy · Sharp/Tangy · Buttery/Creamy · Herbal · Sweet · Salty · Milky/Lactic · Nutty · Fruity · Toasty · Bitter · Caramel · Sour · Moldy/Blue · Robust · Grassy

💬 COMMENTS/SUGGESTIONS

🧀 RATING ☆ ☆ ☆ ☆ ☆

🍷 COMBINED WITH

CHEESE
Tasting

NAME

CREAMERY	AGE
RIND	DATE
ORIGIN	PRICE

🥛 MILK

- ☐ Cow
- ☐ Goat
- ☐ Raw
- ☐ Sheep
- ☐ Buffalo
- ☐ _____

🧀 SMELL & TEXTURE

- ☐ Strong
- ☐ Medium
- ☐ Slight
- ☐ Odorless

- ☐ Runny
- ☐ Soft
- ☐ Semi-soft
- ☐ Semi-firm

- ☐ Firm
- ☐ Hard

📝 NOTES

Appearance: _____
_____
_____
_____

Aroma: _____
_____
_____
_____

Taste: _____
_____
_____
_____

Mouthfeel: _____
_____
_____
_____

😊 FLAVOR WHEEL

Earthy · Sharp/Tangy · Buttery/Creamy · Herbal · Salty · Nutty · Toasty · Caramel · Moldy/Blue · Grassy · Robust · Sour · Bitter · Fruity · Milky/Lactic · Sweet

🧀 RATING ☆☆☆☆☆

🍷 COMBINED WITH

💬 COMMENTS/SUGGESTIONS

CHEESE Tasting

NAME

CREAMERY	AGE
RIND	DATE
ORIGIN	PRICE

🥛 MILK

- ☐ Cow
- ☐ Goat
- ☐ Raw
- ☐ Sheep
- ☐ Buffalo
- ☐ _____

🧀 SMELL & TEXTURE

- ☐ Strong
- ☐ Medium
- ☐ Slight
- ☐ Odorless

- ☐ Runny
- ☐ Soft
- ☐ Semi-soft
- ☐ Semi-firm

- ☐ Firm
- ☐ Hard

📝 NOTES

Appearance:
_____
_____
_____

Aroma:
_____
_____
_____

Taste:
_____
_____
_____

Mouthfeel:
_____
_____
_____

😋 FLAVOR WHEEL

Earthy — Sharp/Tangy — Buttery/Creamy — Herbal — Salty — Nutty — Toasty — Caramel — Moldy/Blue — Grassy — Robust — Sour — Bitter — Fruity — Milky/Lactic — Sweet

👍 RATING ☆☆☆☆☆

🧀 COMBINED WITH

💬 COMMENTS/SUGGESTIONS

CHEESE Tasting

NAME

CREAMERY | **AGE**

RIND | **DATE**

ORIGIN | **PRICE**

🥛 MILK

- ☐ Cow
- ☐ Sheep
- ☐ Goat
- ☐ Buffalo
- ☐ Raw
- ☐ _____

🧀 SMELL & TEXTURE

- ☐ Strong
- ☐ Runny
- ☐ Firm
- ☐ Medium
- ☐ Soft
- ☐ Hard
- ☐ Slight
- ☐ Semi-soft
- ☐ Odorless
- ☐ Semi-firm

📝 NOTES

Appearance: _____
_____
_____
_____

Aroma: _____
_____
_____
_____

Taste: _____
_____
_____
_____

Mouthfeel: _____
_____
_____
_____

😋 FLAVOR WHEEL

Earthy — Sharp/Tangy
Sweet — Buttery/Creamy
Milky/Lactic — Herbal
Fruity — Salty
Bitter — Nutty
Sour — Toasty
Robust — Caramel
Grassy — Moldy/Blue

⭐ RATING | ☆☆☆☆☆

🍷 COMBINED WITH

💬 COMMENTS/SUGGESTIONS

_____
_____
_____
_____
_____
_____
_____
_____
_____
_____
_____

56

CHEESE Tasting

NAME	
CREAMERY	AGE
RIND	DATE
ORIGIN	PRICE

🥛 MILK

- ☐ Cow
- ☐ Sheep
- ☐ Goat
- ☐ Buffalo
- ☐ Raw
- ☐ _____

🧀 SMELL & TEXTURE

- ☐ Strong
- ☐ Medium
- ☐ Slight
- ☐ Odorless

- ☐ Runny
- ☐ Soft
- ☐ Semi-soft
- ☐ Semi-firm

- ☐ Firm
- ☐ Hard

📝 NOTES

Appearance:
_____
_____
_____

Aroma:
_____
_____
_____

Taste:
_____
_____
_____

Mouthfeel:
_____
_____
_____

😊 FLAVOR WHEEL

Earthy · Sharp/Tangy · Buttery/Creamy · Herbal · Salty · Nutty · Toasty · Caramel · Moldy/Blue · Grassy · Robust · Sour · Bitter · Fruity · Milky/Lactic · Sweet

☺ RATING ☆ ☆ ☆ ☆ ☆

🧀 COMBINED WITH

💬 COMMENTS/SUGGESTIONS

CHEESE
Tasting

NAME	
CREAMERY	AGE
RIND	DATE
ORIGIN	PRICE

🥛 MILK

- ☐ Cow
- ☐ Sheep
- ☐ Goat
- ☐ Buffalo
- ☐ Raw
- ☐ _____

🧀 SMELL & TEXTURE

- ☐ Strong
- ☐ Runny
- ☐ Firm
- ☐ Medium
- ☐ Soft
- ☐ Hard
- ☐ Slight
- ☐ Semi-soft
- ☐ Odorless
- ☐ Semi-firm

📝 NOTES

Appearance:
_____
_____
_____

Aroma:
_____
_____
_____

Taste:
_____
_____
_____

Mouthfeel:
_____
_____
_____

😋 FLAVOR WHEEL

Earthy — Sharp/Tangy — Buttery/Creamy — Herbal — Salty — Nutty — Toasty — Caramel — Moldy/Blue — Grassy — Robust — Sour — Bitter — Fruity — Milky/Lactic — Sweet

🧀 RATING ☆☆☆☆☆

🍷 COMBINED WITH

💬 COMMENTS/SUGGESTIONS
_____
_____
_____
_____
_____
_____
_____
_____
_____
_____
_____

58

CHEESE Tasting

NAME	
CREAMERY	AGE
RIND	DATE
ORIGIN	PRICE

🥛 MILK

- ☐ Cow
- ☐ Sheep
- ☐ Goat
- ☐ Buffalo
- ☐ Raw
- ☐ _____

🧀 SMELL & TEXTURE

- ☐ Strong
- ☐ Medium
- ☐ Slight
- ☐ Odorless
- ☐ Runny
- ☐ Soft
- ☐ Semi-soft
- ☐ Semi-firm
- ☐ Firm
- ☐ Hard

📝 NOTES

Appearance:
_____
_____
_____

Aroma:
_____
_____
_____

Taste:
_____
_____
_____
_____

Mouthfeel:
_____
_____
_____

😋 FLAVOR WHEEL

Earthy — Sharp/Tangy — Buttery/Creamy — Herbal — Salty — Nutty — Toasty — Caramel — Moldy/Blue — Grassy — Robust — Sour — Bitter — Fruity — Milky/Lactic — Sweet

👍 RATING | ☆ ☆ ☆ ☆ ☆

🍷 COMBINED WITH

💬 COMMENTS/SUGGESTIONS

_____
_____
_____
_____
_____
_____
_____
_____
_____
_____
_____
_____
_____

CHEESE Tasting

NAME	
CREAMERY	AGE
RIND	DATE
ORIGIN	PRICE

🥛 MILK

- ☐ Cow
- ☐ Sheep
- ☐ Goat
- ☐ Buffalo
- ☐ Raw
- ☐ _____

🧀 SMELL & TEXTURE

- ☐ Strong
- ☐ Runny
- ☐ Firm
- ☐ Medium
- ☐ Soft
- ☐ Hard
- ☐ Slight
- ☐ Semi-soft
- ☐ Odorless
- ☐ Semi-firm

📝 NOTES

Appearance:
_____
_____
_____

Aroma:
_____
_____
_____

Taste:
_____
_____
_____

Mouthfeel:
_____
_____
_____

😋 FLAVOR WHEEL

Earthy, Sharp/Tangy, Buttery/Creamy, Sweet, Herbal, Milky/Lactic, Fruity, Salty, Bitter, Nutty, Sour, Toasty, Robust, Caramel, Grassy, Moldy/Blue

👍 RATING ☆☆☆☆☆

🍷 COMBINED WITH

💬 COMMENTS/SUGGESTIONS
_____
_____
_____
_____
_____
_____
_____
_____
_____
_____
_____

CHEESE
Tasting

NAME

CREAMERY | **AGE**

RIND | **DATE**

ORIGIN | **PRICE**

🥛 MILK

- ☐ Cow   ☐ Sheep
- ☐ Goat   ☐ Buffalo
- ☐ Raw   ☐ _____

🧀 SMELL & TEXTURE

- ☐ Strong   ☐ Runny   ☐ Firm
- ☐ Medium   ☐ Soft   ☐ Hard
- ☐ Slight   ☐ Semi-soft
- ☐ Odorless   ☐ Semi-firm

✍️ NOTES

Appearance: _____
_____
_____
_____

Aroma: _____
_____
_____
_____

Taste: _____
_____
_____
_____

Mouthfeel: _____
_____
_____
_____

😊 FLAVOR WHEEL

Earthy — Sharp/Tangy — Buttery/Creamy
Sweet — Herbal
Milky/Lactic — Salty
Fruity
Bitter — Nutty
Sour — Toasty
Robust — Caramel
Grassy — Moldy/Blue

👍 RATING ☆ ☆ ☆ ☆ ☆

🧀 COMBINED WITH

💬 COMMENTS/SUGGESTIONS

_____
_____
_____
_____
_____
_____
_____
_____
_____
_____
_____
_____
_____
_____
_____
_____

CHEESE
Tasting

NAME		
CREAMERY		**AGE**
RIND		**DATE**
ORIGIN		**PRICE**

🥛 MILK

- ☐ Cow
- ☐ Sheep
- ☐ Goat
- ☐ Buffalo
- ☐ Raw
- ☐ _____

🧀 SMELL & TEXTURE

- ☐ Strong
- ☐ Medium
- ☐ Slight
- ☐ Odorless
- ☐ Runny
- ☐ Soft
- ☐ Semi-soft
- ☐ Semi-firm
- ☐ Firm
- ☐ Hard

📝 NOTES

Appearance:

_____

_____

_____

Aroma:

_____

_____

_____

Taste:

_____

_____

_____

Mouthfeel:

_____

_____

_____

😋 FLAVOR WHEEL

Earthy — Sharp/Tangy — Buttery/Creamy — Herbal — Salty — Nutty — Toasty — Caramel — Moldy/Blue — Grassy — Robust — Sour — Bitter — Fruity — Milky/Lactic — Sweet

⭐ RATING | ☆ ☆ ☆ ☆ ☆

🍷 COMBINED WITH

💬 COMMENTS/SUGGESTIONS

_____

_____

_____

_____

_____

_____

_____

_____

_____

_____

_____

CHEESE *Tasting*

NAME	
CREAMERY	AGE
RIND	DATE
ORIGIN	PRICE

🥛 MILK

- ☐ Cow
- ☐ Sheep
- ☐ Goat
- ☐ Buffalo
- ☐ Raw
- ☐ _____

🧀 SMELL & TEXTURE

- ☐ Strong
- ☐ Medium
- ☐ Slight
- ☐ Odorless
- ☐ Runny
- ☐ Soft
- ☐ Semi-soft
- ☐ Semi-firm
- ☐ Firm
- ☐ Hard

📝 NOTES

Appearance:
_____
_____
_____

Aroma:
_____
_____
_____

Taste:
_____
_____
_____

Mouthfeel:
_____
_____
_____

😋 FLAVOR WHEEL

Earthy · Sharp/Tangy · Buttery/Creamy · Herbal · Salty · Nutty · Toasty · Caramel · Moldy/Blue · Grassy · Robust · Sour · Bitter · Fruity · Milky/Lactic · Sweet

👍 RATING ☆☆☆☆☆

🍷 COMBINED WITH

💬 COMMENTS/SUGGESTIONS

_____
_____
_____
_____
_____
_____
_____
_____
_____
_____
_____
_____
_____

63

CHEESE Tasting

NAME	
CREAMERY	AGE
RIND	DATE
ORIGIN	PRICE

🥛 MILK

- ☐ Cow
- ☐ Sheep
- ☐ Goat
- ☐ Buffalo
- ☐ Raw
- ☐ _____

🧀 SMELL & TEXTURE

- ☐ Strong
- ☐ Runny
- ☐ Firm
- ☐ Medium
- ☐ Soft
- ☐ Hard
- ☐ Slight
- ☐ Semi-soft
- ☐ Odorless
- ☐ Semi-firm

📝 NOTES

Appearance: _____
_____
_____
_____

Aroma: _____
_____
_____
_____

Taste: _____
_____
_____
_____

Mouthfeel: _____
_____
_____
_____

☺ FLAVOR WHEEL

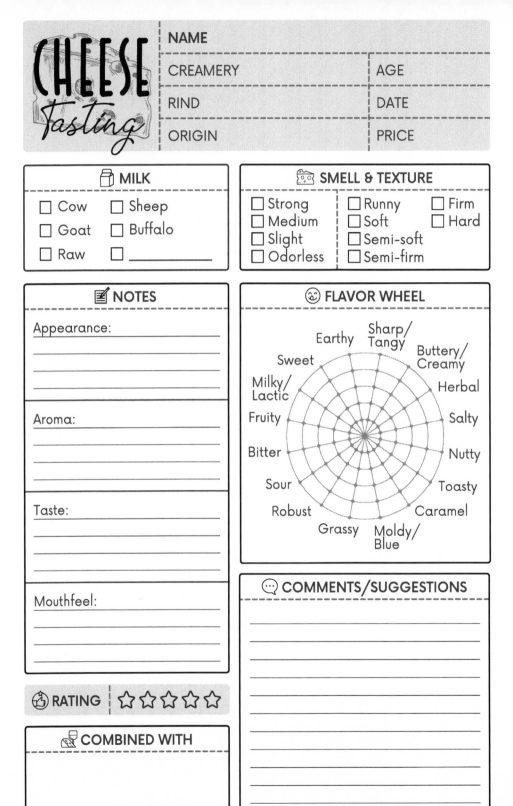

Earthy, Sharp/Tangy, Buttery/Creamy, Sweet, Herbal, Milky/Lactic, Salty, Fruity, Bitter, Nutty, Sour, Toasty, Robust, Caramel, Grassy, Moldy/Blue

💬 COMMENTS/SUGGESTIONS

_____
_____
_____
_____
_____
_____
_____
_____
_____
_____
_____
_____

🏵 RATING ☆☆☆☆☆

🍷 COMBINED WITH

CHEESE Tasting

NAME	
CREAMERY	AGE
RIND	DATE
ORIGIN	PRICE

🥛 MILK

- ☐ Cow
- ☐ Goat
- ☐ Raw
- ☐ Sheep
- ☐ Buffalo
- ☐ _____

🧀 SMELL & TEXTURE

- ☐ Strong
- ☐ Medium
- ☐ Slight
- ☐ Odorless
- ☐ Runny
- ☐ Soft
- ☐ Semi-soft
- ☐ Semi-firm
- ☐ Firm
- ☐ Hard

📝 NOTES

Appearance: _____

Aroma: _____

Taste: _____

Mouthfeel: _____

😋 FLAVOR WHEEL

Earthy — Sharp/Tangy — Buttery/Creamy — Herbal — Salty — Nutty — Toasty — Caramel — Moldy/Blue — Grassy — Robust — Sour — Bitter — Fruity — Milky/Lactic — Sweet

👍 RATING ☆☆☆☆☆

🍷 COMBINED WITH

💬 COMMENTS/SUGGESTIONS

CHEESE Tasting

NAME

CREAMERY	AGE
RIND	DATE
ORIGIN	PRICE

🥛 MILK

- ☐ Cow
- ☐ Sheep
- ☐ Goat
- ☐ Buffalo
- ☐ Raw
- ☐ _____

🧀 SMELL & TEXTURE

- ☐ Strong
- ☐ Medium
- ☐ Slight
- ☐ Odorless
- ☐ Runny
- ☐ Soft
- ☐ Semi-soft
- ☐ Semi-firm
- ☐ Firm
- ☐ Hard

📝 NOTES

Appearance:

_____
_____
_____

Aroma:

_____
_____
_____

Taste:

_____
_____
_____
_____

Mouthfeel:

_____
_____
_____

😋 FLAVOR WHEEL

Earthy
Sharp/Tangy
Buttery/Creamy
Sweet
Herbal
Milky/Lactic
Fruity
Salty
Bitter
Nutty
Sour
Toasty
Robust
Caramel
Grassy
Moldy/Blue

☺ RATING ☆☆☆☆☆

🍷 COMBINED WITH

💬 COMMENTS/SUGGESTIONS

_____
_____
_____
_____
_____
_____
_____
_____
_____
_____
_____
_____

CHEESE Tasting

NAME	
CREAMERY	AGE
RIND	DATE
ORIGIN	PRICE

🥛 MILK

☐ Cow ☐ Sheep
☐ Goat ☐ Buffalo
☐ Raw ☐ _____

🧀 SMELL & TEXTURE

☐ Strong ☐ Runny ☐ Firm
☐ Medium ☐ Soft ☐ Hard
☐ Slight ☐ Semi-soft
☐ Odorless ☐ Semi-firm

📝 NOTES

Appearance:
_____
_____
_____

Aroma:
_____
_____
_____

Taste:
_____
_____
_____

Mouthfeel:
_____
_____
_____

😋 FLAVOR WHEEL

Earthy — Sharp/Tangy
Sweet — Buttery/Creamy
Milky/Lactic — Herbal
Fruity — Salty
Bitter — Nutty
Sour — Toasty
Robust — Caramel
Grassy — Moldy/Blue

💬 COMMENTS/SUGGESTIONS

_____
_____
_____
_____
_____
_____
_____
_____
_____
_____
_____
_____

👍 RATING ☆ ☆ ☆ ☆ ☆

🍷 COMBINED WITH

CHEESE Tasting

NAME	
CREAMERY	AGE
RIND	DATE
ORIGIN	PRICE

🥛 MILK

- ☐ Cow
- ☐ Sheep
- ☐ Goat
- ☐ Buffalo
- ☐ Raw
- ☐ _____

🧀 SMELL & TEXTURE

- ☐ Strong
- ☐ Runny
- ☐ Firm
- ☐ Medium
- ☐ Soft
- ☐ Hard
- ☐ Slight
- ☐ Semi-soft
- ☐ Odorless
- ☐ Semi-firm

📝 NOTES

Appearance:

_____
_____
_____

Aroma:

_____
_____
_____

Taste:

_____
_____
_____

Mouthfeel:

_____
_____
_____

😋 FLAVOR WHEEL

Earthy
Sharp/Tangy
Buttery/Creamy
Sweet
Herbal
Milky/Lactic
Fruity
Salty
Bitter
Nutty
Sour
Toasty
Robust
Caramel
Grassy
Moldy/Blue

👍 RATING ☆☆☆☆☆

🍷 COMBINED WITH

💬 COMMENTS/SUGGESTIONS

_____
_____
_____
_____
_____
_____
_____
_____
_____
_____

CHEESE Tasting

NAME

CREAMERY	AGE
RIND	DATE
ORIGIN	PRICE

🥛 MILK

- [ ] Cow
- [ ] Goat
- [ ] Raw
- [ ] Sheep
- [ ] Buffalo
- [ ] _____

🧀 SMELL & TEXTURE

- [ ] Strong
- [ ] Medium
- [ ] Slight
- [ ] Odorless
- [ ] Runny
- [ ] Soft
- [ ] Semi-soft
- [ ] Semi-firm
- [ ] Firm
- [ ] Hard

📝 NOTES

Appearance:
_____
_____
_____

Aroma:
_____
_____
_____

Taste:
_____
_____
_____
_____

Mouthfeel:
_____
_____
_____

😋 FLAVOR WHEEL

Earthy — Sharp/Tangy — Buttery/Creamy — Herbal — Salty — Nutty — Toasty — Caramel — Moldy/Blue — Grassy — Robust — Sour — Bitter — Fruity — Milky/Lactic — Sweet

👍 RATING ☆☆☆☆☆

🧀 COMBINED WITH

💬 COMMENTS/SUGGESTIONS

_____
_____
_____
_____
_____
_____
_____
_____
_____
_____
_____

CHEESE Tasting

NAME	
CREAMERY	AGE
RIND	DATE
ORIGIN	PRICE

🥛 MILK

- ☐ Cow
- ☐ Goat
- ☐ Raw
- ☐ Sheep
- ☐ Buffalo
- ☐ _____

🧀 SMELL & TEXTURE

- ☐ Strong
- ☐ Medium
- ☐ Slight
- ☐ Odorless
- ☐ Runny
- ☐ Soft
- ☐ Semi-soft
- ☐ Semi-firm
- ☐ Firm
- ☐ Hard

📝 NOTES

Appearance: _____
_____
_____
_____

Aroma: _____
_____
_____
_____

Taste: _____
_____
_____
_____

Mouthfeel: _____
_____
_____
_____

😋 FLAVOR WHEEL

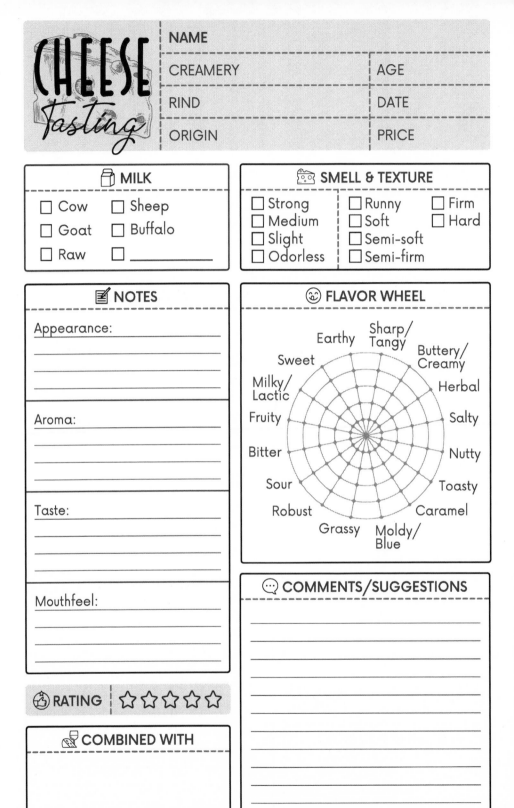

Earthy, Sharp/Tangy, Buttery/Creamy, Sweet, Herbal, Milky/Lactic, Salty, Fruity, Nutty, Bitter, Toasty, Sour, Caramel, Robust, Moldy/Blue, Grassy

🧀 RATING ☆☆☆☆☆

🍷 COMBINED WITH

💬 COMMENTS/SUGGESTIONS

_____
_____
_____
_____
_____
_____
_____
_____
_____
_____
_____

CHEESE *Tasting*

NAME	
CREAMERY	AGE
RIND	DATE
ORIGIN	PRICE

🥛 MILK

- ☐ Cow
- ☐ Goat
- ☐ Raw
- ☐ Sheep
- ☐ Buffalo
- ☐ _____

🧀 SMELL & TEXTURE

- ☐ Strong
- ☐ Medium
- ☐ Slight
- ☐ Odorless

- ☐ Runny
- ☐ Soft
- ☐ Semi-soft
- ☐ Semi-firm

- ☐ Firm
- ☐ Hard

✍️ NOTES

Appearance:
_____
_____
_____

Aroma:
_____
_____
_____

Taste:
_____
_____
_____
_____

Mouthfeel:
_____
_____
_____
_____

😊 FLAVOR WHEEL

Earthy — Sharp/Tangy — Buttery/Creamy
Sweet — Herbal
Milky/Lactic — Salty
Fruity — Nutty
Bitter — Toasty
Sour — Caramel
Robust — Moldy/Blue
Grassy

🧀 RATING | ☆ ☆ ☆ ☆ ☆

🍷 COMBINED WITH

💬 COMMENTS/SUGGESTIONS
_____
_____
_____
_____
_____
_____
_____
_____
_____
_____
_____
_____
_____
_____

CHEESE *Tasting*

NAME	
CREAMERY	AGE
RIND	DATE
ORIGIN	PRICE

🥛 MILK

- ☐ Cow
- ☐ Goat
- ☐ Raw
- ☐ Sheep
- ☐ Buffalo
- ☐ _____

🧀 SMELL & TEXTURE

- ☐ Strong
- ☐ Medium
- ☐ Slight
- ☐ Odorless
- ☐ Runny
- ☐ Soft
- ☐ Semi-soft
- ☐ Semi-firm
- ☐ Firm
- ☐ Hard

📝 NOTES

Appearance:

Aroma:

Taste:

Mouthfeel:

😋 FLAVOR WHEEL

Earthy
Sharp/Tangy
Buttery/Creamy
Sweet
Herbal
Milky/Lactic
Fruity
Salty
Bitter
Nutty
Sour
Toasty
Robust
Caramel
Grassy
Moldy/Blue

🧀 RATING ☆☆☆☆☆

🍷 COMBINED WITH

💬 COMMENTS/SUGGESTIONS

CHEESE Tasting

NAME	
CREAMERY	AGE
RIND	DATE
ORIGIN	PRICE

🥛 MILK

- ☐ Cow
- ☐ Sheep
- ☐ Goat
- ☐ Buffalo
- ☐ Raw
- ☐ _____

🧀 SMELL & TEXTURE

- ☐ Strong
- ☐ Medium
- ☐ Slight
- ☐ Odorless
- ☐ Runny
- ☐ Soft
- ☐ Semi-soft
- ☐ Semi-firm
- ☐ Firm
- ☐ Hard

📝 NOTES

Appearance:
_____
_____
_____

Aroma:
_____
_____
_____

Taste:
_____
_____
_____

Mouthfeel:
_____
_____
_____

😊 FLAVOR WHEEL

Earthy / Sharp/Tangy / Buttery/Creamy / Sweet / Milky/Lactic / Herbal / Fruity / Salty / Bitter / Nutty / Sour / Toasty / Robust / Caramel / Grassy / Moldy/Blue

👍 RATING ☆☆☆☆☆

🍷 COMBINED WITH

💬 COMMENTS/SUGGESTIONS
_____
_____
_____
_____
_____
_____
_____
_____
_____
_____
_____
_____

CHEESE Tasting

NAME

CREAMERY	AGE
RIND	DATE
ORIGIN	PRICE

🥛 MILK

- ☐ Cow
- ☐ Sheep
- ☐ Goat
- ☐ Buffalo
- ☐ Raw
- ☐ _____

🧀 SMELL & TEXTURE

- ☐ Strong
- ☐ Runny
- ☐ Firm
- ☐ Medium
- ☐ Soft
- ☐ Hard
- ☐ Slight
- ☐ Semi-soft
- ☐ Odorless
- ☐ Semi-firm

📝 NOTES

Appearance: _____
_____
_____

Aroma: _____
_____
_____

Taste: _____
_____
_____

Mouthfeel: _____
_____
_____

😋 FLAVOR WHEEL

Earthy — Sharp/Tangy — Buttery/Creamy — Sweet — Herbal — Milky/Lactic — Salty — Fruity — Nutty — Bitter — Toasty — Sour — Caramel — Robust — Moldy/Blue — Grassy

🧀 RATING ☆☆☆☆☆

🍷 COMBINED WITH

💬 COMMENTS/SUGGESTIONS

CHEESE Tasting

NAME		
CREAMERY	AGE	
RIND	DATE	
ORIGIN	PRICE	

🥛 MILK

- ☐ Cow
- ☐ Goat
- ☐ Raw
- ☐ Sheep
- ☐ Buffalo
- ☐ _____

🧀 SMELL & TEXTURE

- ☐ Strong
- ☐ Medium
- ☐ Slight
- ☐ Odorless
- ☐ Runny
- ☐ Soft
- ☐ Semi-soft
- ☐ Semi-firm
- ☐ Firm
- ☐ Hard

📝 NOTES

Appearance:
_____
_____
_____

Aroma:
_____
_____
_____

Taste:
_____
_____
_____
_____

Mouthfeel:
_____
_____
_____

😋 FLAVOR WHEEL

Earthy — Sharp/Tangy — Buttery/Creamy — Herbal — Salty — Nutty — Toasty — Caramel — Moldy/Blue — Grassy — Robust — Sour — Bitter — Fruity — Milky/Lactic — Sweet

💬 COMMENTS/SUGGESTIONS

_____
_____
_____
_____
_____
_____
_____
_____
_____
_____
_____
_____
_____

👍 RATING ☆☆☆☆☆

🍷 COMBINED WITH

CHEESE Tasting

NAME		
CREAMERY	AGE	
RIND	DATE	
ORIGIN	PRICE	

🥛 MILK

- ☐ Cow
- ☐ Sheep
- ☐ Goat
- ☐ Buffalo
- ☐ Raw
- ☐ _____

🧀 SMELL & TEXTURE

- ☐ Strong
- ☐ Medium
- ☐ Slight
- ☐ Odorless
- ☐ Runny
- ☐ Soft
- ☐ Semi-soft
- ☐ Semi-firm
- ☐ Firm
- ☐ Hard

📝 NOTES

Appearance:

_____
_____
_____

Aroma:

_____
_____
_____

Taste:

_____
_____
_____
_____

Mouthfeel:

_____
_____
_____

😋 FLAVOR WHEEL

Earthy · Sharp/Tangy · Buttery/Creamy · Herbal · Salty · Nutty · Toasty · Caramel · Moldy/Blue · Grassy · Robust · Sour · Bitter · Fruity · Milky/Lactic · Sweet

👍 RATING ☆☆☆☆☆

🍷 COMBINED WITH

💬 COMMENTS/SUGGESTIONS

_____
_____
_____
_____
_____
_____
_____
_____
_____
_____
_____
_____

CHEESE *Tasting*

NAME	
CREAMERY	AGE
RIND	DATE
ORIGIN	PRICE

🥛 MILK

- ☐ Cow ☐ Sheep
- ☐ Goat ☐ Buffalo
- ☐ Raw ☐ _____

🧀 SMELL & TEXTURE

- ☐ Strong ☐ Runny ☐ Firm
- ☐ Medium ☐ Soft ☐ Hard
- ☐ Slight ☐ Semi-soft
- ☐ Odorless ☐ Semi-firm

📝 NOTES

Appearance:
_____
_____
_____

Aroma:
_____
_____
_____

Taste:
_____
_____
_____

Mouthfeel:
_____
_____
_____

😋 FLAVOR WHEEL

Earthy · Sharp/Tangy · Buttery/Creamy · Herbal · Salty · Nutty · Toasty · Caramel · Moldy/Blue · Grassy · Robust · Sour · Bitter · Fruity · Milky/Lactic · Sweet

👍 RATING ☆☆☆☆☆

🍷 COMBINED WITH

💬 COMMENTS/SUGGESTIONS

_____
_____
_____
_____
_____
_____
_____
_____
_____
_____
_____
_____
_____

CHEESE Tasting

NAME

CREAMERY | **AGE**

RIND | **DATE**

ORIGIN | **PRICE**

🥛 MILK

- [ ] Cow
- [ ] Goat
- [ ] Raw
- [ ] Sheep
- [ ] Buffalo
- [ ] _____

🧀 SMELL & TEXTURE

- [ ] Strong
- [ ] Medium
- [ ] Slight
- [ ] Odorless
- [ ] Runny
- [ ] Soft
- [ ] Semi-soft
- [ ] Semi-firm
- [ ] Firm
- [ ] Hard

📝 NOTES

Appearance:
_____
_____
_____

Aroma:
_____
_____
_____

Taste:
_____
_____
_____

Mouthfeel:
_____
_____
_____

😋 FLAVOR WHEEL

Earthy, Sharp/Tangy, Buttery/Creamy, Sweet, Herbal, Milky/Lactic, Fruity, Salty, Bitter, Nutty, Sour, Toasty, Robust, Caramel, Grassy, Moldy/Blue

💬 COMMENTS/SUGGESTIONS

🧀 RATING ☆☆☆☆☆

🍷 COMBINED WITH

CHEESE Tasting

NAME		
CREAMERY	AGE	
RIND	DATE	
ORIGIN	PRICE	

🥛 MILK

- ☐ Cow
- ☐ Sheep
- ☐ Goat
- ☐ Buffalo
- ☐ Raw
- ☐ _____

🧀 SMELL & TEXTURE

- ☐ Strong
- ☐ Medium
- ☐ Slight
- ☐ Odorless
- ☐ Runny
- ☐ Soft
- ☐ Semi-soft
- ☐ Semi-firm
- ☐ Firm
- ☐ Hard

📝 NOTES

Appearance: _____

Aroma: _____

Taste: _____

Mouthfeel: _____

😋 FLAVOR WHEEL

Earthy, Sharp/Tangy, Buttery/Creamy, Sweet, Herbal, Milky/Lactic, Fruity, Salty, Bitter, Nutty, Sour, Toasty, Robust, Caramel, Grassy, Moldy/Blue

👍 RATING ☆☆☆☆☆

🧀🍷 COMBINED WITH

💬 COMMENTS/SUGGESTIONS

CHEESE Tasting

NAME	
CREAMERY	AGE
RIND	DATE
ORIGIN	PRICE

🥛 MILK

- ☐ Cow
- ☐ Sheep
- ☐ Goat
- ☐ Buffalo
- ☐ Raw
- ☐ _____

🧀 SMELL & TEXTURE

- ☐ Strong
- ☐ Medium
- ☐ Slight
- ☐ Odorless
- ☐ Runny
- ☐ Soft
- ☐ Semi-soft
- ☐ Semi-firm
- ☐ Firm
- ☐ Hard

📝 NOTES

Appearance: _____
_____
_____
_____

Aroma: _____
_____
_____
_____

Taste: _____
_____
_____
_____

Mouthfeel: _____
_____
_____
_____

😋 FLAVOR WHEEL

Earthy, Sharp/Tangy, Buttery/Creamy, Herbal, Salty, Nutty, Toasty, Caramel, Moldy/Blue, Grassy, Robust, Sour, Bitter, Fruity, Milky/Lactic, Sweet

😊 RATING ☆☆☆☆☆

🍷 COMBINED WITH

💬 COMMENTS/SUGGESTIONS

_____
_____
_____
_____
_____
_____
_____
_____
_____
_____
_____
_____

CHEESE Tasting

NAME		
CREAMERY		AGE
RIND		DATE
ORIGIN		PRICE

🥛 MILK

- ☐ Cow
- ☐ Sheep
- ☐ Goat
- ☐ Buffalo
- ☐ Raw
- ☐ _____

🧀 SMELL & TEXTURE

- ☐ Strong
- ☐ Runny
- ☐ Firm
- ☐ Medium
- ☐ Soft
- ☐ Hard
- ☐ Slight
- ☐ Semi-soft
- ☐ Odorless
- ☐ Semi-firm

✍️ NOTES

Appearance:
_____
_____
_____

Aroma:
_____
_____
_____

Taste:
_____
_____
_____

Mouthfeel:
_____
_____
_____

😋 FLAVOR WHEEL

Earthy — Sharp/Tangy — Buttery/Creamy — Herbal — Salty — Nutty — Toasty — Caramel — Moldy/Blue — Grassy — Robust — Sour — Bitter — Fruity — Milky/Lactic — Sweet

🧀 RATING | ☆ ☆ ☆ ☆ ☆

🍷 COMBINED WITH

💬 COMMENTS/SUGGESTIONS

_____
_____
_____
_____
_____
_____
_____
_____
_____
_____
_____
_____

CHEESE Tasting

NAME		
CREAMERY		AGE
RIND		DATE
ORIGIN		PRICE

🥛 MILK

- ☐ Cow
- ☐ Sheep
- ☐ Goat
- ☐ Buffalo
- ☐ Raw
- ☐ _____

🧀 SMELL & TEXTURE

- ☐ Strong
- ☐ Runny
- ☐ Firm
- ☐ Medium
- ☐ Soft
- ☐ Hard
- ☐ Slight
- ☐ Semi-soft
- ☐ Odorless
- ☐ Semi-firm

📝 NOTES

Appearance:
_____
_____
_____

Aroma:
_____
_____
_____

Taste:
_____
_____
_____

Mouthfeel:
_____
_____
_____

😋 FLAVOR WHEEL

Earthy · Sharp/Tangy · Buttery/Creamy · Herbal · Salty · Nutty · Toasty · Caramel · Moldy/Blue · Grassy · Robust · Sour · Bitter · Fruity · Milky/Lactic · Sweet

😋 RATING ☆☆☆☆☆

🍷 COMBINED WITH

💬 COMMENTS/SUGGESTIONS

_____
_____
_____
_____
_____
_____
_____
_____
_____
_____

CHEESE Tasting

NAME		
CREAMERY	AGE	
RIND	DATE	
ORIGIN	PRICE	

🥛 MILK

- ☐ Cow ☐ Sheep
- ☐ Goat ☐ Buffalo
- ☐ Raw ☐ _____

🧀 SMELL & TEXTURE

☐ Strong	☐ Runny	☐ Firm
☐ Medium	☐ Soft	☐ Hard
☐ Slight	☐ Semi-soft	
☐ Odorless	☐ Semi-firm	

📝 NOTES

Appearance:
_____
_____
_____

Aroma:
_____
_____
_____

Taste:
_____
_____
_____

Mouthfeel:
_____
_____
_____

😋 FLAVOR WHEEL

Earthy
Sharp/Tangy
Buttery/Creamy
Sweet
Milky/Lactic
Herbal
Fruity
Salty
Bitter
Nutty
Sour
Toasty
Robust
Caramel
Grassy
Moldy/Blue

👍 RATING ☆☆☆☆☆

🍷 COMBINED WITH

💬 COMMENTS/SUGGESTIONS

_____
_____
_____
_____
_____
_____
_____
_____
_____
_____
_____
_____
_____

CHEESE Tasting

NAME

CREAMERY	AGE
RIND	DATE
ORIGIN	PRICE

🥛 MILK

- ☐ Cow
- ☐ Sheep
- ☐ Goat
- ☐ Buffalo
- ☐ Raw
- ☐ _____

🧀 SMELL & TEXTURE

- ☐ Strong
- ☐ Runny
- ☐ Firm
- ☐ Medium
- ☐ Soft
- ☐ Hard
- ☐ Slight
- ☐ Semi-soft
- ☐ Odorless
- ☐ Semi-firm

📝 NOTES

Appearance: _____
_____
_____
_____

Aroma: _____
_____
_____
_____

Taste: _____
_____
_____
_____

Mouthfeel: _____
_____
_____
_____

😋 FLAVOR WHEEL

Earthy — Sharp/Tangy — Buttery/Creamy
Sweet — Herbal
Milky/Lactic — Salty
Fruity — Nutty
Bitter — Toasty
Sour — Caramel
Robust — Grassy — Moldy/Blue

👍 RATING ☆☆☆☆☆

🧀 COMBINED WITH

💬 COMMENTS/SUGGESTIONS

CHEESE Tasting

NAME		
CREAMERY	AGE	
RIND	DATE	
ORIGIN	PRICE	

🥛 MILK

- ☐ Cow
- ☐ Sheep
- ☐ Goat
- ☐ Buffalo
- ☐ Raw
- ☐ _____

🧀 SMELL & TEXTURE

- ☐ Strong
- ☐ Medium
- ☐ Slight
- ☐ Odorless
- ☐ Runny
- ☐ Soft
- ☐ Semi-soft
- ☐ Semi-firm
- ☐ Firm
- ☐ Hard

📝 NOTES

Appearance: _____
_____
_____
_____

Aroma: _____
_____
_____
_____

Taste: _____
_____
_____
_____

Mouthfeel: _____
_____
_____
_____

😋 FLAVOR WHEEL

Earthy · Sharp/Tangy · Buttery/Creamy · Herbal · Salty · Nutty · Toasty · Caramel · Moldy/Blue · Grassy · Robust · Sour · Bitter · Fruity · Milky/Lactic · Sweet

🧀 RATING ☆☆☆☆☆

🧀 COMBINED WITH

💬 COMMENTS/SUGGESTIONS

CHEESE Tasting

NAME		
CREAMERY		AGE
RIND		DATE
ORIGIN		PRICE

🥛 MILK

- ☐ Cow
- ☐ Sheep
- ☐ Goat
- ☐ Buffalo
- ☐ Raw
- ☐ _____

🧀 SMELL & TEXTURE

- ☐ Strong
- ☐ Medium
- ☐ Slight
- ☐ Odorless
- ☐ Runny
- ☐ Soft
- ☐ Semi-soft
- ☐ Semi-firm
- ☐ Firm
- ☐ Hard

📝 NOTES

Appearance:
_____
_____
_____

Aroma:
_____
_____
_____

Taste:
_____
_____
_____

Mouthfeel:
_____
_____
_____

😋 FLAVOR WHEEL

Earthy · Sharp/Tangy · Buttery/Creamy · Sweet · Herbal · Milky/Lactic · Salty · Fruity · Nutty · Bitter · Toasty · Sour · Caramel · Robust · Moldy/Blue · Grassy

☺ RATING ☆☆☆☆☆

🍷 COMBINED WITH

💬 COMMENTS/SUGGESTIONS
_____
_____
_____
_____
_____
_____
_____
_____
_____
_____

CHEESE Tasting

NAME		
CREAMERY		AGE
RIND		DATE
ORIGIN		PRICE

🥛 MILK

- ☐ Cow
- ☐ Goat
- ☐ Raw
- ☐ Sheep
- ☐ Buffalo
- ☐ _____

🧀 SMELL & TEXTURE

- ☐ Strong
- ☐ Medium
- ☐ Slight
- ☐ Odorless
- ☐ Runny
- ☐ Soft
- ☐ Semi-soft
- ☐ Semi-firm
- ☐ Firm
- ☐ Hard

📝 NOTES

Appearance:
_____
_____
_____

Aroma:
_____
_____
_____

Taste:
_____
_____
_____

Mouthfeel:
_____
_____
_____

😋 FLAVOR WHEEL

Earthy · Sharp/Tangy · Buttery/Creamy · Herbal · Salty · Nutty · Toasty · Caramel · Moldy/Blue · Grassy · Robust · Sour · Bitter · Fruity · Milky/Lactic · Sweet

💬 COMMENTS/SUGGESTIONS

_____
_____
_____
_____
_____
_____
_____
_____
_____
_____
_____
_____
_____

🧀 RATING ☆ ☆ ☆ ☆ ☆

🍷 COMBINED WITH

CHEESE
Tasting

NAME

CREAMERY	AGE
RIND	DATE
ORIGIN	PRICE

🥛 MILK

- ☐ Cow
- ☐ Goat
- ☐ Raw
- ☐ Sheep
- ☐ Buffalo
- ☐ _____

🧀 SMELL & TEXTURE

- ☐ Strong
- ☐ Medium
- ☐ Slight
- ☐ Odorless

- ☐ Runny
- ☐ Soft
- ☐ Semi-soft
- ☐ Semi-firm

- ☐ Firm
- ☐ Hard

📝 NOTES

Appearance:
_____
_____
_____

Aroma:
_____
_____
_____

Taste:
_____
_____
_____

Mouthfeel:
_____
_____
_____

😋 FLAVOR WHEEL

Earthy, Sharp/Tangy, Buttery/Creamy, Herbal, Salty, Nutty, Toasty, Caramel, Moldy/Blue, Grassy, Robust, Sour, Bitter, Fruity, Milky/Lactic, Sweet

🏅 RATING | ☆☆☆☆☆

🍷 COMBINED WITH

💬 COMMENTS/SUGGESTIONS

_____
_____
_____
_____
_____
_____
_____
_____
_____
_____

CHEESE
Tasting

NAME		
CREAMERY		AGE
RIND		DATE
ORIGIN		PRICE

🥛 MILK

- ☐ Cow
- ☐ Sheep
- ☐ Goat
- ☐ Buffalo
- ☐ Raw
- ☐ _____

🧀 SMELL & TEXTURE

- ☐ Strong
- ☐ Medium
- ☐ Slight
- ☐ Odorless
- ☐ Runny
- ☐ Soft
- ☐ Semi-soft
- ☐ Semi-firm
- ☐ Firm
- ☐ Hard

📝 NOTES

Appearance: _____

Aroma: _____

Taste: _____

Mouthfeel: _____

😋 FLAVOR WHEEL

Earthy Sharp/Tangy
Sweet Buttery/Creamy
Milky/Lactic Herbal
Fruity Salty
Bitter Nutty
Sour Toasty
Robust Caramel
Grassy Moldy/Blue

🧀 RATING ☆ ☆ ☆ ☆ ☆

🍷 COMBINED WITH

💬 COMMENTS/SUGGESTIONS

CHEESE Tasting

NAME		
CREAMERY	**AGE**	
RIND	**DATE**	
ORIGIN	**PRICE**	

🥛 MILK

- ☐ Cow
- ☐ Sheep
- ☐ Goat
- ☐ Buffalo
- ☐ Raw
- ☐ _____

🧀 SMELL & TEXTURE

- ☐ Strong
- ☐ Runny
- ☐ Firm
- ☐ Medium
- ☐ Soft
- ☐ Hard
- ☐ Slight
- ☐ Semi-soft
- ☐ Odorless
- ☐ Semi-firm

📝 NOTES

Appearance:
_____
_____
_____

Aroma:
_____
_____
_____

Taste:
_____
_____
_____

Mouthfeel:
_____
_____
_____

😋 FLAVOR WHEEL

Earthy — Sharp/Tangy — Buttery/Creamy — Herbal — Salty — Nutty — Toasty — Caramel — Moldy/Blue — Grassy — Robust — Sour — Bitter — Fruity — Milky/Lactic — Sweet

⭐ RATING ☆☆☆☆☆

🍷 COMBINED WITH

💬 COMMENTS/SUGGESTIONS
_____
_____
_____
_____
_____
_____
_____
_____
_____
_____

CHEESE *Tasting*

NAME		
CREAMERY		AGE
RIND		DATE
ORIGIN		PRICE

🥛 MILK

- ☐ Cow
- ☐ Sheep
- ☐ Goat
- ☐ Buffalo
- ☐ Raw
- ☐ _____

🧀 SMELL & TEXTURE

- ☐ Strong
- ☐ Medium
- ☐ Slight
- ☐ Odorless
- ☐ Runny
- ☐ Soft
- ☐ Semi-soft
- ☐ Semi-firm
- ☐ Firm
- ☐ Hard

📝 NOTES

Appearance: _____
_____
_____
_____

Aroma: _____
_____
_____
_____

Taste: _____
_____
_____
_____

Mouthfeel: _____
_____
_____
_____

😋 FLAVOR WHEEL

Earthy · Sharp/Tangy · Buttery/Creamy · Herbal · Salty · Nutty · Toasty · Caramel · Moldy/Blue · Grassy · Robust · Sour · Bitter · Fruity · Milky/Lactic · Sweet

😊 RATING ☆☆☆☆☆

🍷 COMBINED WITH

💬 COMMENTS/SUGGESTIONS

CHEESE Tasting

NAME	
CREAMERY	AGE
RIND	DATE
ORIGIN	PRICE

🥛 MILK

- ☐ Cow
- ☐ Goat
- ☐ Raw
- ☐ Sheep
- ☐ Buffalo
- ☐ _____

🧀 SMELL & TEXTURE

- ☐ Strong
- ☐ Medium
- ☐ Slight
- ☐ Odorless
- ☐ Runny
- ☐ Soft
- ☐ Semi-soft
- ☐ Semi-firm
- ☐ Firm
- ☐ Hard

📝 NOTES

Appearance: _____
_____
_____
_____

Aroma: _____
_____
_____
_____

Taste: _____
_____
_____
_____

Mouthfeel: _____
_____
_____
_____

😋 FLAVOR WHEEL

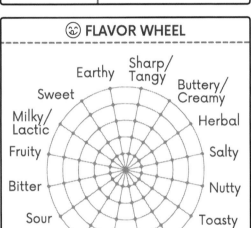

Earthy · Sharp/Tangy · Buttery/Creamy · Sweet · Herbal · Milky/Lactic · Salty · Fruity · Bitter · Nutty · Sour · Toasty · Robust · Caramel · Grassy · Moldy/Blue

🧀 RATING ☆☆☆☆☆

🍷 COMBINED WITH

💬 COMMENTS/SUGGESTIONS

CHEESE Tasting

NAME	
CREAMERY	AGE
RIND	DATE
ORIGIN	PRICE

🥛 MILK

- ☐ Cow
- ☐ Goat
- ☐ Raw
- ☐ Sheep
- ☐ Buffalo
- ☐ _____

🧀 SMELL & TEXTURE

- ☐ Strong
- ☐ Medium
- ☐ Slight
- ☐ Odorless

- ☐ Runny
- ☐ Soft
- ☐ Semi-soft
- ☐ Semi-firm

- ☐ Firm
- ☐ Hard

📝 NOTES

Appearance: _____

Aroma: _____

Taste: _____

Mouthfeel: _____

😊 FLAVOR WHEEL

Earthy — Sharp/Tangy — Buttery/Creamy — Herbal — Salty — Nutty — Toasty — Caramel — Moldy/Blue — Grassy — Robust — Sour — Bitter — Fruity — Milky/Lactic — Sweet

👍 RATING   ☆ ☆ ☆ ☆ ☆

🍷 COMBINED WITH

💬 COMMENTS/SUGGESTIONS

CHEESE
Tasting

NAME		
CREAMERY		AGE
RIND		DATE
ORIGIN		PRICE

🥛 MILK

- ☐ Cow
- ☐ Goat
- ☐ Raw
- ☐ Sheep
- ☐ Buffalo
- ☐ _____

🧀 SMELL & TEXTURE

- ☐ Strong
- ☐ Medium
- ☐ Slight
- ☐ Odorless
- ☐ Runny
- ☐ Soft
- ☐ Semi-soft
- ☐ Semi-firm
- ☐ Firm
- ☐ Hard

📝 NOTES

Appearance: _____

_____

_____

_____

Aroma: _____

_____

_____

_____

Taste: _____

_____

_____

_____

_____

Mouthfeel: _____

_____

_____

_____

😋 FLAVOR WHEEL

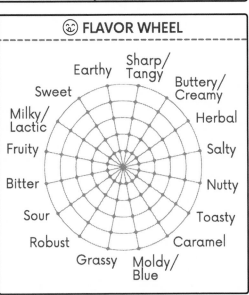

Earthy · Sharp/Tangy · Buttery/Creamy · Sweet · Herbal · Milky/Lactic · Salty · Fruity · Nutty · Bitter · Toasty · Sour · Caramel · Robust · Grassy · Moldy/Blue

💬 COMMENTS/SUGGESTIONS

_____

_____

_____

_____

_____

_____

_____

_____

_____

_____

_____

_____

🧀 RATING ☆☆☆☆☆

🍷 COMBINED WITH

CHEESE *Tasting*

NAME		
CREAMERY		AGE
RIND		DATE
ORIGIN		PRICE

🥛 MILK

- [ ] Cow
- [ ] Goat
- [ ] Raw
- [ ] Sheep
- [ ] Buffalo
- [ ] _____

🧀 SMELL & TEXTURE

- [ ] Strong
- [ ] Medium
- [ ] Slight
- [ ] Odorless
- [ ] Runny
- [ ] Soft
- [ ] Semi-soft
- [ ] Semi-firm
- [ ] Firm
- [ ] Hard

📝 NOTES

Appearance: _____
_____
_____
_____

Aroma: _____
_____
_____
_____

Taste: _____
_____
_____
_____

Mouthfeel: _____
_____
_____
_____

😋 FLAVOR WHEEL

Earthy / Sharp/Tangy / Buttery/Creamy / Herbal / Salty / Nutty / Toasty / Caramel / Moldy/Blue / Grassy / Robust / Sour / Bitter / Fruity / Milky/Lactic / Sweet

💬 COMMENTS/SUGGESTIONS

_____
_____
_____
_____
_____
_____
_____
_____
_____
_____
_____
_____
_____
_____
_____
_____
_____

👍 RATING ☆ ☆ ☆ ☆ ☆

🍷 COMBINED WITH

CHEESE Tasting

NAME	
CREAMERY	AGE
RIND	DATE
ORIGIN	PRICE

🥛 MILK

- ☐ Cow
- ☐ Sheep
- ☐ Goat
- ☐ Buffalo
- ☐ Raw
- ☐ _____

🧀 SMELL & TEXTURE

- ☐ Strong
- ☐ Medium
- ☐ Slight
- ☐ Odorless
- ☐ Runny
- ☐ Soft
- ☐ Semi-soft
- ☐ Semi-firm
- ☐ Firm
- ☐ Hard

📝 NOTES

Appearance:
_____
_____
_____

Aroma:
_____
_____
_____

Taste:
_____
_____
_____

Mouthfeel:
_____
_____
_____

😋 FLAVOR WHEEL

Earthy, Sharp/Tangy, Buttery/Creamy, Sweet, Herbal, Milky/Lactic, Salty, Fruity, Bitter, Nutty, Sour, Toasty, Robust, Caramel, Grassy, Moldy/Blue

🧀 RATING ☆☆☆☆☆

🍷 COMBINED WITH

💬 COMMENTS/SUGGESTIONS

_____
_____
_____
_____
_____
_____
_____
_____
_____
_____
_____

CHEESE Tasting

NAME		
CREAMERY	AGE	
RIND	DATE	
ORIGIN	PRICE	

🥛 MILK

- [ ] Cow
- [ ] Goat
- [ ] Raw
- [ ] Sheep
- [ ] Buffalo
- [ ] _____

🧀 SMELL & TEXTURE

- [ ] Strong
- [ ] Medium
- [ ] Slight
- [ ] Odorless

- [ ] Runny
- [ ] Soft
- [ ] Semi-soft
- [ ] Semi-firm

- [ ] Firm
- [ ] Hard

📝 NOTES

Appearance: _____
_____
_____
_____

Aroma: _____
_____
_____
_____

Taste: _____
_____
_____
_____

Mouthfeel: _____
_____
_____
_____

😋 FLAVOR WHEEL

Earthy · Sharp/Tangy · Buttery/Creamy · Herbal · Salty · Nutty · Toasty · Caramel · Moldy/Blue · Grassy · Robust · Sour · Bitter · Fruity · Milky/Lactic · Sweet

👍 RATING ☆☆☆☆☆

🧀 COMBINED WITH

💬 COMMENTS/SUGGESTIONS

_____
_____
_____
_____
_____
_____
_____
_____
_____
_____
_____
_____
_____

CHEESE Tasting

NAME		
CREAMERY		AGE
RIND		DATE
ORIGIN		PRICE

🥛 MILK

- ☐ Cow
- ☐ Sheep
- ☐ Goat
- ☐ Buffalo
- ☐ Raw
- ☐ _____

🧀 SMELL & TEXTURE

- ☐ Strong
- ☐ Runny
- ☐ Firm
- ☐ Medium
- ☐ Soft
- ☐ Hard
- ☐ Slight
- ☐ Semi-soft
- ☐ Odorless
- ☐ Semi-firm

📝 NOTES

Appearance:
_____
_____
_____

Aroma:
_____
_____
_____

Taste:
_____
_____
_____

Mouthfeel:
_____
_____
_____

😋 FLAVOR WHEEL

Earthy, Sharp/Tangy, Buttery/Creamy, Sweet, Herbal, Milky/Lactic, Fruity, Salty, Bitter, Nutty, Sour, Toasty, Robust, Caramel, Grassy, Moldy/Blue

🏅 RATING ☆☆☆☆☆

🍷 COMBINED WITH

💬 COMMENTS/SUGGESTIONS
_____
_____
_____
_____
_____
_____
_____
_____
_____
_____

CHEESE Tasting

NAME		
CREAMERY	AGE	
RIND	DATE	
ORIGIN	PRICE	

🥛 MILK

- ☐ Cow
- ☐ Sheep
- ☐ Goat
- ☐ Buffalo
- ☐ Raw
- ☐ _____

🧀 SMELL & TEXTURE

- ☐ Strong
- ☐ Medium
- ☐ Slight
- ☐ Odorless
- ☐ Runny
- ☐ Soft
- ☐ Semi-soft
- ☐ Semi-firm
- ☐ Firm
- ☐ Hard

✍️ NOTES

Appearance:
_____
_____
_____

Aroma:
_____
_____
_____

Taste:
_____
_____
_____

Mouthfeel:
_____
_____
_____

😊 FLAVOR WHEEL

Earthy, Sharp/Tangy, Buttery/Creamy, Sweet, Herbal, Milky/Lactic, Salty, Fruity, Nutty, Bitter, Toasty, Sour, Caramel, Robust, Moldy/Blue, Grassy

👍 RATING ☆☆☆☆☆

🍷 COMBINED WITH

💬 COMMENTS/SUGGESTIONS
_____
_____
_____
_____
_____
_____
_____
_____
_____
_____
_____
_____

NAME

CREAMERY	AGE
RIND	DATE
ORIGIN	PRICE

🥛 MILK

- ☐ Cow
- ☐ Sheep
- ☐ Goat
- ☐ Buffalo
- ☐ Raw
- ☐ _____

🧀 SMELL & TEXTURE

- ☐ Strong
- ☐ Medium
- ☐ Slight
- ☐ Odorless
- ☐ Runny
- ☐ Soft
- ☐ Semi-soft
- ☐ Semi-firm
- ☐ Firm
- ☐ Hard

📝 NOTES

Appearance: _____

_____

_____

_____

Aroma: _____

_____

_____

_____

Taste: _____

_____

_____

_____

Mouthfeel: _____

_____

_____

_____

😋 FLAVOR WHEEL

Earthy · Sharp/Tangy · Buttery/Creamy
Sweet · Herbal
Milky/Lactic · Salty
Fruity · Nutty
Bitter · Toasty
Sour · Caramel
Robust · Moldy/Blue
Grassy

🧀 RATING ☆☆☆☆☆

🍷 COMBINED WITH

💬 COMMENTS/SUGGESTIONS

_____

_____

_____

_____

_____

_____

_____

_____

_____

_____

_____

_____

CHEESE
Tasting

NAME		
CREAMERY		AGE
RIND		DATE
ORIGIN		PRICE

🥛 MILK

- ☐ Cow
- ☐ Sheep
- ☐ Goat
- ☐ Buffalo
- ☐ Raw
- ☐ _____

🧀 SMELL & TEXTURE

- ☐ Strong
- ☐ Medium
- ☐ Slight
- ☐ Odorless
- ☐ Runny
- ☐ Soft
- ☐ Semi-soft
- ☐ Semi-firm
- ☐ Firm
- ☐ Hard

📝 NOTES

Appearance: _____

Aroma: _____

Taste: _____

Mouthfeel: _____

😊 FLAVOR WHEEL

Earthy
Sharp/Tangy
Sweet
Buttery/Creamy
Milky/Lactic
Herbal
Fruity
Salty
Bitter
Nutty
Sour
Toasty
Robust
Caramel
Grassy
Moldy/Blue

👍 RATING ☆☆☆☆☆

🧀 COMBINED WITH

💬 COMMENTS/SUGGESTIONS

CHEESE
Tasting

NAME

CREAMERY | **AGE**

RIND | **DATE**

ORIGIN | **PRICE**

🥛 MILK

- ☐ Cow
- ☐ Goat
- ☐ Raw
- ☐ Sheep
- ☐ Buffalo
- ☐ _____

🧀 SMELL & TEXTURE

- ☐ Strong
- ☐ Medium
- ☐ Slight
- ☐ Odorless
- ☐ Runny
- ☐ Soft
- ☐ Semi-soft
- ☐ Semi-firm
- ☐ Firm
- ☐ Hard

📝 NOTES

Appearance:
_____
_____
_____

Aroma:
_____
_____
_____

Taste:
_____
_____
_____

Mouthfeel:
_____
_____
_____

😋 FLAVOR WHEEL

Earthy — Sharp/Tangy — Buttery/Creamy
Sweet — Herbal
Milky/Lactic — Salty
Fruity
Bitter — Nutty
Sour — Toasty
Robust — Caramel
Grassy — Moldy/Blue

🧀 RATING ☆☆☆☆☆

🍷 COMBINED WITH

💬 COMMENTS/SUGGESTIONS
_____
_____
_____
_____
_____
_____
_____
_____
_____
_____
_____
_____

CHEESE Tasting

NAME		
CREAMERY	AGE	
RIND	DATE	
ORIGIN	PRICE	

🥛 MILK

- ☐ Cow
- ☐ Sheep
- ☐ Goat
- ☐ Buffalo
- ☐ Raw
- ☐ _____

🧀 SMELL & TEXTURE

- ☐ Strong
- ☐ Runny
- ☐ Firm
- ☐ Medium
- ☐ Soft
- ☐ Hard
- ☐ Slight
- ☐ Semi-soft
- ☐ Odorless
- ☐ Semi-firm

📝 NOTES

Appearance:
_____
_____
_____

Aroma:
_____
_____
_____

Taste:
_____
_____
_____

Mouthfeel:
_____
_____
_____

😋 FLAVOR WHEEL

Earthy, Sharp/Tangy, Buttery/Creamy, Sweet, Herbal, Milky/Lactic, Fruity, Salty, Bitter, Nutty, Sour, Toasty, Robust, Caramel, Grassy, Moldy/Blue

💬 COMMENTS/SUGGESTIONS

_____
_____
_____
_____
_____
_____
_____
_____
_____
_____
_____
_____
_____

👍 RATING ☆☆☆☆☆

🍷 COMBINED WITH

CHEESE
Tasting

NAME	
CREAMERY	AGE
RIND	DATE
ORIGIN	PRICE

🥛 MILK

- ☐ Cow
- ☐ Sheep
- ☐ Goat
- ☐ Buffalo
- ☐ Raw
- ☐ _____

🧀 SMELL & TEXTURE

- ☐ Strong
- ☐ Runny
- ☐ Firm
- ☐ Medium
- ☐ Soft
- ☐ Hard
- ☐ Slight
- ☐ Semi-soft
- ☐ Odorless
- ☐ Semi-firm

📝 NOTES

Appearance:

_____
_____
_____

Aroma:

_____
_____
_____

Taste:

_____
_____
_____

Mouthfeel:

_____
_____
_____

😊 FLAVOR WHEEL

Earthy · Sharp/Tangy · Buttery/Creamy · Herbal · Salty · Nutty · Toasty · Caramel · Moldy/Blue · Grassy · Robust · Sour · Bitter · Fruity · Milky/Lactic · Sweet

💬 COMMENTS/SUGGESTIONS

_____
_____
_____
_____
_____
_____
_____
_____
_____
_____
_____

🐭 RATING ☆☆☆☆☆

🍷 COMBINED WITH